Quality Time for Quality Kids

Second printing 1993

Quality Times for Quality Kids
Copyright © 1992 Glenn Smith and Kathy Tomberlin

All rights reserved. Printed in the United States of America. No part of this book may be used or reproduced in any manner whatsoever without written permission except in the case of brief quotations embodied in critical articles or reviews. For information, address New View Publications, P.O. Box 3021, Chapel Hill, N.C. 27515-3021.

Illustrations by Jeffrey Hale
Edited by S.J. Font
Desktop Publishing by Rafaela Padilla

ISBN 0-944337-09-0
Library of Congress Catalog Card Number: 92-50331

For information regarding speaking engagements by the authors, contact New View Publications.

Quantity Purchases

Companies, professional groups, clubs, and other organizations may qualify for special terms when ordering quantities of this title. For information contact the Sales Department, New View Publications, P.O. Box 3021, Chapel Hill, N.C. 27515-3021.

Manufactured in the United States of America.

Quality Time
for
Quality Kids

Glenn Smith
Kathy Tomberlin

New View Publications
Chapel Hill

Introduction

This workbook was inspired by *In Pursuit of Happiness* (1987), a self-help book written by Perry Good, Senior Faculty Member of the Institute for Reality Therapy. Her book sets in motion the concepts presented by Dr. William Glasser's books *Control Theory* (1980) and *Reality Therapy* (1965). In 1989 Robert Sullo took these same concepts and wrote *Teach Them To Be Happy*, a guide for presenting Control Theory to children.

After years of facilitating groups for children, we have compiled the activities that have had the most success helping our young students and clients build self-esteem. Through helping children experience Control Theory concepts, including the ideas of personal choice, basic needs, perception, and total behavior, we can help children understand the value of themselves and others.

Although we cannot take credit for originating all of these activities, we will accept credit for coordinating them and transforming these ideas into activities to help children learn about their internal motivation and behavior.

We would like to extend a special thanks to the Monroe School counselors and the Family Connection therapists who have captured the essence of these ideas and created something special for children. A very special thanks to Cindy Van Camp, Lynn Jauch, Teralee Baines, Gayle Polk, Daryl Hines, Dr. Bob Bowman, and Perry Good for their suggestions. Finally, we are grateful to all the parents and children who have trusted us enough to allow us to learn from them.

Glenn Smith
Kathy Tomberlin

Contents

❶ The Process   1

❷ The Activities   16

Section A
Involvement and Group Solidarity   17

Guess Who?   18
Toilet Paper Game   20
Buddy Collage   23
Buddy Mobile   25
Cheers   28
Mix and Mingle   30
Name Games   33
Quality Interview   36

Section B
Affirmation of Self   39

Quality Accessories   40
The Thumbbodys   43
Smile Bingo   45
Musical Compliments   47
Do Like - Don't Like Collage   50
Quality Clothespins   53
Star Search   56
Read All About It!   59

Section C
Affirmation of Others   62

Balloon Game   63
Giant Pictures   66
Pats On The Back   69
Mailbox Game   71
Happy Letters   74

Need-Fulfilling Ornaments   77
The Helping Game   80

Section D
Learning About Oneself and Others   83

Quality Star Puzzles   84
Pictures Ablowing   87
Which Are You?   90
Me Collage   93
Happy Mobiles   96
Paper Bag Puppets   99
Cookie Bears   101
Happy Books   103

Section E
Feeling, Thinking, and Doing Behaviors   106

Flush that Stinkin' Thinkin'   107
Happy Sad Collage   109
Alligator River   112
I was so Mad!   115
Total Behavior Game   118

Section F
Problem Solving   121

The Brain Game   122
Freedom Finder Planes   125
Super Hero Cartoons   128
The Risk Takers   131
Attack   133

❸ The Resources   136

The Process

What Is Control Theory?

Control Theory maintains that all human beings have genetic instructions, or basic needs, built into our cerebral cortex which motivate behavior and help us survive both physically and psychologically. Control Theory psychology professes that all behavior is motivated by powerful forces inside ourselves (a "control system"). This is quite different from the conventional belief of stimulus-response psychology, which contends that behavior is determined by forces outside of ourselves (a stimuli). William Glasser, MD., author of *Control Theory. A New Explanation Of How We Control Our Lives*, writes:

> ... nothing we do is caused by what happens outside of us. In fact, everything we do — good or bad, effective or ineffective, painful or pleasurable, crazy or sane, sick or well, drunk or sober — is to satisfy powerful forces within ourselves.

In short, Control Theory helps define responsibility. Through understanding what we can control, we can begin to take more effective control of our lives.

Control Theory And Children

According to Robert Sullo, a child psychologist, faculty member at the Institute for Reality Therapy, and author of *Teach Them To Be Happy*, Control Theory can be taught to people of any age. He states:

> ...these ideas and concepts can be applied successfully with children as young as two years old, but only if the child's development level is taken into consideration and the process applied accordingly. It is perfectly appropriate for you to ask a two-year-old child to think.

How does one address variance of developmental levels? It is our experience that most child education centers around two styles of teaching. One teaching style is selected for a "cognitive" child in which educators introduce new ideas or concepts to the children. A second teaching style is "experiential" in which educators use exercises through which children learn concepts by participating. It is not enough to implement one of these styles into your group; there needs to be an integration of both styles.

It is important to introduce children to the Control Theory ideas to help them understand the true meaning of the word *responsibility.* In a world that assumes that behavior is controlled outside of oneself, it is too common to believe that we are only victims of circumstance with little or no control of our present or our future.

Control Theory encourages individuals to look within themselves for the solutions for their fulfillment. Children who take responsibility for effectively acting on the world, instead of reacting to the world, are in an excellent position to attain quality in their lives.

The activities in this manual are designed to help you introduce to children, both on an experiential and cognitive level, what it really means to attain happiness. The activities invite children to experience what it feels like to satisfy their basic needs, and then encourage children to think about their behavior choices and how those choices contribute to meeting their needs.

Introducing Children To The Five Basic Needs

Control Theory contends that there are a series of instructions, or basic needs, built into our cerebral cortex. One set of instructions centers around our physical well-being; another set addresses our psychological well-being. Dr. Glasser classifies these basic needs into five categories: survival, love or belonging, power, fun, and freedom.

1. Survival

Our survival needs tell us what we have to do to keep alive and well. Have you ever wondered what would happen if our bodies did not thirst or hunger? We would most definitely dehydrate or starve. What would happen if we did not get any sleep, were not able to detect cold or hot, or did not have the desire to reproduce? If these instructions were not programmed into our minds and bodies we would not survive. It is important to introduce children to their survival needs and the significance of learning to meet them long-term.

2. Love or Belonging

All individuals have the basic need to belong, to share, to cooperate, to be connected to someone. According to our genetic instructions, we have no choice but to search out relationships and maintain them. The basic need for love or belonging is so strong that many individuals choose to endure painful experiences to hold onto their relationships. Think about the battered child that still wants to go home, or the young person who chooses destructive behaviors to be part of a group. Also, think about how good it feels to be with someone you care about and who cares about you. We believe that educators and counselors should invite children to learn about their love or belonging need and encourage them to take steps toward finding agreeable persons to satisfy this need.

3. Power

We all have the basic need for importance, self-worth, a say in how things are done. We want to know that we matter and that we can contribute. The word *power* may convey some negative pictures because this basic need is often abused. People have satisfied this need by choosing to exercise control over other people, or by using their position for their own gain. In a more positive vein, one can also choose to meet the need for power by striving for recognition. Think about when you received an award, got good grades, excelled in sports or received a promotion. Educators and counselors should help children learn about their basic need for power, help them explore their options, and encourage them to determine which choices will be gratifying.

4. Fun

We all have the basic need for fun in our lives. Dr. Glasser explains that fun is the genetic reward for learning. Fun, like power, can be abused. Some people choose to meet this need by making fun of others or by abusing themselves. People also meet their need for fun in responsible ways, such as hobbies, sports, shopping, reading, playing, socializing, and learning. Do you remember how much fun you had learning to ride a bike? Think about how your life would be if you weren't allowed to do things for fun. It is important for children to be introduced to appropriate ways to meet their need for fun.

5. Freedom

Also within our genetic framework is our basic need for freedom. The constitution of the United States supports our need for freedom by stating that certain freedoms are inalienable rights. Our freedom need can be demonstrated through our desire to move around. If you were tied to your chair right now and could not move, you would experience the need for freedom. Our freedom need is also evident through our desire to make our own choices. Just say the word "NO" and watch what happens. We recommend that educators, counselors, and parents assist children in effectively dealing with their freedom need. Help children to explore their options and identify the consequences, both positive and negative, that accompany each choice.

The Need-fulfilling Group

Control Theory contends that basic needs did not happen by accident. Our basic needs were developed early in our history. Those persons who best learned to cooperate long term (love and fun), and to compete long term (power and freedom), were those who were able to survive. Today, the people who can best get along with others capability to depend on themselves, seem to live happier, healthier lives.

It is possible to introduce children to their basic needs, both experientially and cognitively, through facilitating a need-fulfilling group. The need fulfilling group invites children to:

• affirm themselves and others, which helps children satisfy their need for power,

• participate at their will, make choices, and express ideas, which introduces children to ways to meet their need for freedom,

• connect with others, to share about things that are important, and work on projects together, which introduces children to ways to fulfill their basic need for love or belonging,

• participate in activities that are experiential and non-threatening, which introduces children to ways of fulfilling their basic need for fun.

Pictures In Our Quality Worlds

Control Theory maintains that our basic needs are all the same but our wants or our pictures of how to satisfy these needs are unique and special. For example, a child may meet his or her need for fun by riding a bike and another might choose to meet the same need by creating an art project. One child might satisfy the need for power through excelling on a sports team and another may fulfill that need by getting good grades in school.

"Different strokes for different folks" was Sly Stone's way of saying we all have unique pictures in our quality worlds. According to Dr. Glasser, our quality worlds are where we store all the pictures that we believe will satisfy one or more of our basic needs. Control Theory contends that it is these pictures in our quality worlds that motivate all of our

behavior and choices. We always want to satisfy these pictures in the real world.

If we have a picture in our heads of how to meet a particular need and we get what we wanted, then we say our picture has been matched. Matched pictures in our quality worlds feel wonderful! Dr. Glasser explains that when the pictures in our heads do not match with what is happening in the external world, we experience frustration and pain. We then try desperately to find a way to ease the pain by attempting new behaviors, both effective and ineffective, adding new pictures to our quality worlds, or giving up.

It is our job as educators, parents, and counselors to introduce children to their options to help them find a match to the unique pictures in their quality worlds.

Self-evaluation and the Quality World

Exploring their quality worlds will not only facilitate children's awareness of themselves, but also will help you become a picture in this special world. If, and only if, you can become part of a child's quality world you will have a chance to motivate their behavior. (It is possible to coerce a child if you are a person with authority and there is a picture in the child's quality world of himself wanting to stay away from unfavorable consequences.) Introducing children to self-evaluation will accelerate their developmental process. You can help by asking questions that encourage them to evaluate their own capabilities.

For example, a child brought to a group a report card with one "A," three "B's" and one "C." Well intentioned, one facilitator said to the child, "Gee, I bet you are proud of that 'A'!" The child smiled but did not say anything. A second facilitator, who understands Control Theory and who wanted to understand this child's quality world asked, "What is it about that report card that means the most to you?" The child beamed and exclaimed, "A 'B' in Social Studies! I worked hard in that class."

The facilitator could have continued to explore this child's quality world by asking more questions, such as, "Were any other grades of value to you?", "What does hard work mean to you?", or "Which class would you choose to work harder in next time?" Below are questions we believe can assist facilitators in helping children acquaint themselves with their quality worlds. Notice how these questions tie directly into the child's basic needs and their pictures.

- What do you want? What is really important to you?
- What needs help you get what you want?
- What choices are you making to help you get what you want?
- What choices do you need to make to help you get what you want?
- If you got your want, what could you do then that you can't do now?
- Until you get what you really want, is there any way you could get some of what you want today?

Encourage children to ask *themselves* the same questions. They will learn to understand that they have basic needs but that there are infinite ways they can satisfy these needs. As the Rolling Stones, a popular rock group, sing, *"You can't always get what you want, but if you try sometime, you just might find, you get what you need."*

Learning About Perceptions

Our basic needs and our pictures are not the only factors that motivate us internally. Our perceptions, or how we view the world, influence the choices that we make. Our perceptions are developed from what we know and what we value. Dr. Glasser believes that, in order to help children develop, knowledge of how our perceptual system works is essential. He writes that we:

… must try to understand that clients act upon the information that is in their own perceived world.

… Beauty is in the eye of the beholder, and so, of course, are ugliness, genius, greatness, and meanness. All our values, good and bad, come from within ourselves. In the real world, where everything exists, there are no values, labels, or designations of any kind.

At an early age a child begins to develop perceptions of themselves and others. A popular adage, "Children Live What They Learn," depicts this idea:

If a child lives with hostility he learns to fight.
If a child lives with criticism he learns to condemn.
If a child lives with ridicule he learns to be shy.
If a child lives with shame he learns to feel guilty.
If a child lives with tolerance he learns to be patient.
If a child lives with encouragement he learns confidence.
If a child lives with praise he learns to appreciate.
If a child lives with fairness he learns justice.
If a child lives with serenity he learns to have faith.
If a child lives with approval he learns to like himself.
If a child lives with acceptance and friendship he learns to find love.

As a group facilitator, it is important to realize that all perceptual systems can be expanded. Applying both an experiential and cognitive component, the activities in this manual help children expand how they perceive themselves and others.

Total Behavior and the Learning Process

You have been introduced to how to help children learn about the pictures in our quality worlds and what happens when the pictures in our heads do not match with input from the outside world. You have also been introduced to how important it is for a facilitator to add new information to the perceptual system. By understanding total behavior you will be in a better position to help children learn how to get what they want.

Control Theory contends that there are four components of behavior that move together in one direction. Control Theory further suggests that each of us has the ability to *control* our total behavior or the direction in which these behaviors are moving. The four components that make up our total behavior are:

Actions   Everything we do, including what we say

Thinking   All the thoughts in our heads, both positive and negative

Physiology All of the electro-biochemical processes in the body

Feeling   All of our sensations generated from how we choose to think and act

Of these four components we can only completely control our actions. Thinking is also directly under our control but this cognitive skill takes quite a bit of discipline and practice. We can gain control of our feelings and physiology only by thought and action. It is impossible to directly change a feeling without changing what one is thinking or doing.

The activities presented in this manual are designed to deal with different learning styles and our understanding of total behavior. Many children have difficulty integrating cognitive or thinking ideas into their perceptual systems. Through the experiential or action component of the activities children can experience or feel the ideas you want to introduce. For those children who are proficient, the discussions, Happywork assignments, and the Happy Journal will help them understand why these activities help them feel good.

Group Process With Children

The group can be an effective means of helping children satisfy all of their basic needs. The group can act as a safe place for children to develop listening skills, to learn about themselves and others, to develop leadership skills, and their special qualities. Facilitating a group can be rewarding. Presented are some ideas that may be helpful in developing your group.

Recognize the Power of Puppets

Children love puppets. Children feel safe around them and will share information with them that they would never share with an adult. Ask the children to bring their favorite puppet from home or ask them to help you make puppets (see the Paper Bag Puppets activity). You could ask the group to help you make a puppet stage out of a refrigerator box and coordinate activities around creating the props you need for puppet shows. Your puppets can facilitate entire groups, introduce new ideas, or take on specific problems and ask the children to help them find solutions.

Keep Groups Small

Divide the group into smaller groups of five or six children. There are creative ways you can do this. Invite children to draw a number out of a hat or count off to form the groups. You can also have them select a card with a particular animal on it. Ask them to make the sound that animal makes until they find all similar animals who make up their group.

Choose a Leader

Choose a leader for each activity to help you coordinate the activity. Leaders can assist with gathering materials, leading discussions, bringing refreshments from home, or doing extra Happywork and sharing it with the group. This helps children develop leadership skills. Ask the smaller groups to find out: "Who is the tallest?", "Who is the oldest?", "Who has the most siblings?", "Who got up the earliest?", etc. When they find out the answer, that person would be the leader for that activity. For the next activity use another question to find a new leader.

Choose a Buddy

We recommend that for the duration of your group each child has a buddy. The buddy is a person that another child could check in with from time to time to share what they are learning. The buddy system can further be used to break up the groups even smaller so children can concentrate. The buddy system also discourages the tendency for some children to be excluded.

Be Consistent

Act on all input from children in a similar manner. Children feel they are important if you treat them equally. Use terms such as, "Thank you for sharing," or "Would you like to add anything else?"

Present Guidelines

Guidelines should be set at the beginning of each group. For example:

- One person may talk at a time
- Respect yourself and others
- Respect property
- Time out procedure guidelines
- Activity choices
- Consequences for irresponsible behavior

Focus On Friendship

Introduce the children to "friendship-making skills". Explain that there are different ways that they can make friends in the group, such as:

- Find out about one another by asking questions
- Don't make fun of others
- Respect differences as well as similarities
- Listen to one another

Establish a Time Out Procedure

Time out can be a constructive system to incorporate into your group. Time out is not a punitive procedure and can be a skill that children learn to use as they get older. Ask children to go to a designated area for a short period of time if they believe they are not contributing effectively to the group. As the group leader, you may have to initiate the procedure and ask children to decide if they need time out. Some options you can offer children who are choosing to disrupt and have not yet learned to remove themselves are:

- To stay in the group and participate responsibly
- To participate in another activity that will not disrupt the group
- To remove themselves to time out until they think they are ready to return and participate responsibly
- To keep disrupting the group and accept the stated consequence (the consequences were determined when the guidelines were set)

Create Choices

Choices are important! Anytime you can create choices, do it! The choices of materials, activities, Happywork, and consequences, are all choices you can create. The group will be need-fulfilling if you have choices!

Affirm Group Members' Similarities and Differences

If a particular child's input is confusing or different from others', take the opportunity to talk about the merits of standing alone or of having unique perceptions. If their input is similar to that of someone else, acknowledge the connection. If you disagree, ask the group what they think. Encourage children to give their opinions and to respect all ideas. Effective questions to ask that may help affirm both similarities and differences are:

- Did anyone hear any group members who liked the same things?
- Does it feel good when others like the same thing you like?
- Did anyone hear any group members who liked something different from the rest of the group?
- Is it OK to like things that are different from what someone else likes?
- Would you do something irresponsible because others did it?

Implement the Family Gram and Happywork

The success of your group may be determined by the extent of family involvement you can promote. The concepts you present in your group should not stay in the group setting. The Family Gram is a note that explains the concepts the child was introduced to in their group that day. By sending home a Family Gram, parents or guardians can take part in what their child is learning. Children should be encouraged to practice what they learned outside of the group, especially with their families. Encourage the children to do Happywork after each activity. Completing it with a family member helps promote family involvement. Also, the use of a Happy Journal is recommended to record the exercises (see the Happy Journal activity.)

Happy Journal

Integrating the skills it takes to become happier takes a lot of practice. The Happy Journal encourages children to integrate the ideas they learn into their daily lives. It provides a written account of how they are learning to take effective control of their lives and it is an effective tool for children to record what they learn from their Happywork. Your job as a group leader or teacher is to first introduce ideas in an experiential, creative way, and then to encourage children to practice them. To make the Happy Journals, follow the same guidelines outlined in the Happy Books activity in this manual. Encourage the children to decorate their Happy Journals any way they want. They take about 15 minutes to make, and can be used with any activity in this manual.

Happy Journal Choices

Happy File: Ask children to decorate a file folder any way they want. Encourage children to place inside special things that show their accomplishments or describe them in a positive way. The file can be used to accumulate information obtained through their Happywork practice. This file could be named "I'm Special", "I'm Wonderful", "I'm Terrific", etc. Encourage children to get their Happy File and look at it from time to time.

Open Journals: The purpose of the Open Journal is to allow group members, group leaders, and parents to communicate in writing those things they perceive that a child is doing which is worthwhile. Set aside the journals in an accessible location and encourage children to read them daily, weekly, etc. This can be an effective medium for group leaders to give affirmative feedback to children when they make effective choices.

Bragging Rights: A few moments each day, encourage the children to BRAG about those accomplishments that they have experienced since the last time the group was together. Every time someone "brags" about a success, encourage the other group members to cheer. Bragging Rights could also be implemented as a time for children to read their Happy Journals, Happy Files, or Open Journals.

Happywork: As with any activity, send home a Family Gram to explain the purpose of the Happy Journal. Encourage journal writing at home. Ask family members to write in the journals or read them with their child.

(The Happy Journal concept was conceived and revised from an idea presented in Perry Good's manual *The Happy Hour Guide*. New View Publications, 1989)

The Activities

Involvement and Group Solidarity

Guess Who?

Purpose To get to know each other in a fun, non-threatening way

Materials Index cards, pencils, small box with numbers (1-50) written on small pieces of paper inside, list of Guess Who? questions

Time 20 minutes

INSTRUCTIONS

Invite children to form groups of four to five and choose a group leader. (For ideas on assembling groups, refer to the Process Section.) Give each group a list of the Guess Who? questions in the Resource Section. Ask each child to draw four numbers out of the box.

Ask group members to find the questions that match their numbers and write the questions and their answer on a separate index card. When they are finished, ask them to give all four index cards to the group leader.

Ask group leaders to randomly read aloud each question and answer. It is the task of the group to Guess Who? the answer belongs.

DISCUSSION

When beginning a group, it is important to offer opportunities for children to get to know each other in fun, non-threatening ways. This activity is also a chance for you to discuss how difficult it is for everyone to meet new people. We recommend that you take this time to discuss how we are all different, but somewhat the same. Similarities and differences could be discussed further, as well as how these make us special.

CHOICES

If you would like to introduce the basic needs, gear questions toward how children choose to satisfy their needs.

Using the buddy system, encourage partners to ask each other all of the questions on the Guess Who? list. Invite buddies to tell the rest of the group some things they learned about their new friend.

HAPPYWORK

Send home a Family Gram that explains the guidelines and purpose of this activity. Encourage children to take questions home, choosing at least five to ask family members. Encourage the interviewers to write the answers in their Happy Journals. (Guess Who? could be played at home if several family members participate.)

Toilet Paper Game

Purpose To appreciate our differences as well as our similarities

Materials Rolls of toilet paper

Time 1 to 5 minutes per person

INSTRUCTIONS

Ask the children to sit in a circle. You may want to keep groups at about five children each. (For ideas for assembling groups, refer to the Process Section.)

Pass around a roll of toilet paper and ask children to take what they need. Some children will choose to take a small amount and others will choose a large amount.

For each square that they take, ask children to share something about themselves that other group members would not know unless they were told. You may find it necessary to help some children by asking them questions for every piece of Toilet Paper they have.

We recommend that you participate by taking lots of squares and sharing about yourself.

DISCUSSION

This activity is an opportunity to encourage involvement in your new group. It is a valuable experience for children to learn that all people are special in their own ways. Control Theory confirms this through its explanation of how we develop individual pictures and place them into our Quality Worlds. Control Theory goes on to explain that it is these pictures that make each of us unique. It is through exploring these quality pictures that we can truly understand one another. Ask children to share one thing that they learned about each person in their group.

CHOICES

After children have taken what they need, ask them specific questions until all the Toilet Paper is gone. Gear questions around specific topics, such as the basic needs (LOVE, POWER, FUN, FREEDOM), signals, family members, etc.

Ask each child to share a problem that they have with the group and ask them to think about what choices they have. Ask them to challenge themselves to think of a choice for each section of Toilet Paper they took.

HAPPYWORK

Ask children to play the Toilet Paper Game with a family member. Ask them to tell their family member to take what they need. Encourage children to ask their family member to share something about themselves for each piece of paper they chose. Ask children to record what they learned about the other person in their Happy Journal and invite them to share with the group. If they need assistance in writing, suggest that they ask for help. Remember to send home a Family Gram to help family members appreciate the purpose of this project.

✎ **Notes**

Buddy Collage

Purpose To demonstrate how our basic needs motivate us in our everyday lives

Materials Construction paper, markers, scissors, magazines, glue

Time 45 minutes for making collages, presentation, and discussion

INSTRUCTIONS

Ask each group member to choose a buddy and to write their buddy's name in big letters on a sheet of construction paper.

Encourage each buddy to share their common interests, common activities, favorite foods with each other.

Ask buddies to write those things that they have in common on their Buddy Collages. Another option is to encourage buddies to look through magazines, cut out, and paste pictures on construction paper in which both share an interest. Invite them to share these collages with the group.

DISCUSSION

For groups to become truly invested in and receptive to new ideas, group members need to be involved with each other. The buddy system is an excellent way to encourage children to get to know each other in a non-threatening way. The buddy system encourages children to check in with one special person from time to time to share what they are learning. The buddy system also discourages the tendency for some children to be excluded. The buddy system can further be used to break the groups up even smaller, so children can concentrate. As with the other involvement activities, it is essential to emphasize that our needs are similar but our pictures are unique.

CHOICES

Group Collage: Invite the entire group to write all their names on a large sheet of construction paper. Encourage the group to find shared interests and activities that they all like which can be included on the paper.

HAPPYWORK

Family Collage: Encourage children to take their collages home to share with their families. Send a Family Gram explaining the purpose of the collages and invite family members to participate with their child in making a Family Collage. Encourage children to share their collages with their group.

Buddy Mobile

Purpose   To explore the unique ways we choose to fulfill our basic needs

Materials   Construction paper, markers, hole puncher, yarn, clothes hangers

Time   30 minutes for creating mobiles, 15 minutes for presentation and discussion

INSTRUCTIONS

Draw six inch circles on colored sheets of construction paper. Ask children to choose a buddy and to cut out several circles.

Ask each pair of buddies to write on their mutual circles the answers to a series of questions. Examples of questions may be:

- How many brothers or sisters do you have?
- What is your favorite activity?
- What is something you do really well?
- What is your favorite food?
- What is your favorite school subject?
- What is your favorite music?

After buddies finish writing the answers to the questions on their shared circles, ask the partners to punch holes at the top of their circles, attach the circles to each other with yarn, and then attach the yarn to clothes hangers. Encourage children to tell about their Buddy Mobiles to the rest of the group.

DISCUSSION

This is another activity that effectively uses the buddy system (see Buddy Collage). The collages and mobiles can be displayed for future reference. The mobiles are a visible description of this child's quality world. Encourage children to explore all the mobiles that are displayed and pick out similarities as well as differences. Point out how similarities meet our need for belonging and how differences meet our need for freedom. At this time you may want to take the opportunity to discuss the importance of accepting others' differences and similarities.

CHOICES

Group Mobiles: Encourage the group to find shared interests and activities that they all like which can be included on a mobile.

Buddy Banners: With construction paper, markers, paper tubes from paper towels, and clothes hangers, ask buddies to make a banner with pictures and cut-outs about their lives. Encourage children to include hobbies, interests, etc. Staple or tape the finished banner to a paper tube or to a wire clothes hanger. Tie yarn to both ends and hang the banner for all to see. Other choices are a Group Banner, Family Banner, or Me Banner. (Time: 45 minutes)

HAPPYWORK

Family Mobile: Encourage children to take their mobiles home to share with their families. Send a Family Gram explaining the purpose of the mobiles and invite family members to participate with their child in making a Family Mobile. Encourage children to share their mobiles with their group.

✎ Notes

Cheers

Purpose To build unity among the group members

Materials Ideas for Cheers, video camera or tape player (optional)

Time 45 minutes to develop Cheers, practice, and demonstrate

INSTRUCTIONS

Divide children into groups no larger than five. Invite children to develop a Cheer about their group or ask them to practice a Cheer that you have originated. (See Resource Section.)

Encourage children to include claps, jumps, and other cheer leading maneuvers. In a large room or outside, invite children to demonstrate their Cheer.

DISCUSSION

This exercise introduces children to traits that are positive and that demonstrate their worth as well as what it takes to work well as a team. Present to the group that a team must believe in themselves, and that each Cheer demonstrates this conviction.

CHOICES

Instead of cheers, ask the children to make up songs, raps, rhymes, or poems.

HAPPYWORK

Encourage children to develop a cheer, song, rap, rhyme, or poem with their families and record it in their Happy Journals. Send home a Family Gram to help parents understand the aim of this activity. Invite children to share their new Family Cheers with their group members.

✎ Notes

Mix and Mingle

Purpose   To share pictures in our quality worlds with other group members

Materials   A list of discussion topics which the group leader will create, tape player with fun music

Time   5 minutes per question

INSTRUCTIONS

Ask children to stand up and gather in the center of the room.

Say "Mix and Mingle."

Turn the tape player on. Encourage the children to walk around the room whispering "Mix and Mingle." Turn off the music and call out a number such as 2,3,4 etc. Ask children to form groups consisting of that number, preferably with the children they are closest to in the room at that time.

While in the groups, ask group members to talk about pictures in their quality world. Topics could be:

- Say something you've done well in school today.
- Say something that you do for fun.
- Talk about a choice you made today that worked.
- Tell about someone who loves you and someone you love.

You might want to ask children to talk about fun things such as your favorite ice cream, pizza, place to go, etc.

DISCUSSION

We recommend that the leader also "Mix and Mingle" with the group and talk about these topics. After this exercise, tell the children that what they were sharing with their group members ties directly into the four basic needs (LOVE, POWER, FUN, and FREEDOM). Also, it may be appropriate to let children share what they have learned about others. This will tie in directly with children's basic need for belonging.

CHOICES

Think of new topics and questions that demonstrate pictures in their quality worlds.

Group Mingle: When working with older children, ask them to stay in one group and talk about all the topics that you present, one topic at a time. When they are through, ask them to write down one thing they remember about each group member. Invite children to tell the rest of the group what they learned about each of their new buddies. (Time: 45 minutes)

Buddy Mingle: Ask children to choose a buddy and to talk about all the topics that you present, one topic at a time. When they are through, ask them to write down at least two things they remember about their new buddy. Invite children to introduce their buddy to the rest of the group. (Time: 45 minutes)

HAPPYWORK

Send home a Family Gram to explain the purpose of this activity. Ask children to ask someone in their family at least two of the questions that were asked in their groups. Ask them to write down what their family members said in their Happy Journal. Give them the opportunity to share with the group when they return.

✎ **Notes**

Name Games

Purpose   To introduce the importance of our names and our families

Materials   Construction paper, small squares (to make letters for names), glue, glitter, stickers, cloth, colored rice, markers

Time   30 minutes to construct name pictures, 3 minutes for each child to present their name

INSTRUCTIONS

Give each child enough construction paper squares to write each letter of their name.

Ask children to decorate each letter of their name any way they choose using the materials provided.

Ask children to paste the squares on a larger sheet of paper entitled, "A SPECIAL NAME FOR A SPECIAL PERSON". It is important to model by doing your own name, decorating it, and presenting information about your name to the group.

DISCUSSION

Children love to hear their names. Through decorating their name, we are inviting children to learn how special they are. Encourage children to research specific questions about their names with their family. Questions they could ask are:

- Where did our last name originate?
- Where did the idea for my first name came from?
- Where are some places our family has lived?
- What are some accomplishments of which our family is proud (graduations, sports, skills, family ideals or traits, etc.)?

This activity helps children meet their needs for belonging and power. We recommend that you research the children's backgrounds in your group to help them work through any confusion over special family situations such as single parent families, blended families, or foster families.

CHOICES

Use the buddy system and ask children to share what they find out about their families with each other.

34

Name Poster: Ask all the children in the group to print the first initial of their names really big on the left side of a large sheet of paper. Ask the group to challenge themselves to describe in five minutes all the positive words that begin with the first initial of their name. List these positive words and phrases on the paper next to the initial. Display for all to see. (Time: 5 minutes per child.)

HAPPYWORK

Coat Of Arms: Encourage children to take home the coat of arms from the Resource Section and present it to their families. Explain in a Family Gram the purpose of the Name Game and include directions. Encourage family members to answer the following questions, by drawing on a picture, design or symbol their own Coat of Arms. Invite family members to decorate it with crayons, markers, or magazine pictures. Questions are:

- What is your greatest personal achievement?
- What is your family's greatest achievement?
- What is one thing you choose to do for fun?
- What is something you need to improve?
- If you could go anywhere, where would you go?
- Who loves you and who do you love?

 Notes

Quality Interview

Purpose To add new pictures to our quality worlds of what it takes to be successful

Materials Happy Journal, paper and pencils, flip chart

Time 15 minutes to prepare for interview, 5 minutes for each child to share with the group

INSTRUCTIONS

Ask children to think of someone they picture as successful and to share what they perceive about people who are successful.

Ask children what behaviors successful people have had to choose, both thinking and doing, to become successful. List behaviors on a flip chart or blackboard.

Present children with a list of questions they can ask the successful person they have been picturing in their minds. Ask each child to write the questions in their Happy Journal and leave space for the answers. Examples of questions:

- When you were a kid, what did you want to be?
- Who did you look up to or admire?
- What choices did you make that helped?
- Who are some people that helped you?
- What are the qualities of a successful person?
- What is one thing of which you are the most proud?

DISCUSSION

Children at a young age have already started to develop perceptions of the world. It is our job to help children explore these perceptions and help them find new information to add. Quality Interviews can be a powerful learning activity that can be used to help children explore their perceptions on a number of issues or personality traits. This activity can also help you introduce the idea that we can change our perceptions about anything if we add new information.

CHOICES

Ask the children to conduct a Quality Interview with individuals who they perceive as happy, confident, smart, or motivated. These people could be teachers, family members, friends, or older children. Encourage children to share what they learned with the group. Depending on the developmental level of the group, this may be an appropriate time to discuss how specific concepts of Control Theory relate to successful people.

Ask children to conduct a Quality Interview with a buddy or with other group members. This a good activity to help group members become more involved. Involvement activities such as Mix and Mingle, Toilet Paper Game, Buddy Collage, Buddy Mobile, or the Name Games can be integrated with this activity.

Quality Interviews can also be incorporated with the Read All About It activity. Use this activity with children with high motivation and high developmental levels.

HAPPYWORK

Encourage and prepare children to conduct a Quality Interview with family members. Send a Family Gram home to explain the purpose of this activity. Ask children to list their questions and the replies in their Happy Journals. Give each child the choice to share their interview with the group.

✎ **Notes**

Affirmation of Self

Quality Accessories

Purpose To introduce positive self-evaluation

Materials Construction paper, scissors, markers, crayons, tape, stapler, glue, and glitter

Time 45 minutes for making accessories, presentation, and discussion

INSTRUCTIONS

Invite children to come together and brainstorm about themselves. List the statements on a flip chart or blackboard for all to see.

After all the affirmations have been listed, ask the children to collect the materials they will need to make their Quality Accessories.

Encourage children to make the accessories of their choice, list positive statements about themselves on their creations, and wear them for all to see. (See Choices for a listing of Quality Accessories.)

DISCUSSION

Often the way we choose to perceive ourselves is the way we will be perceived by others. This activity is useful in encouraging children to look at what they are doing and how they are already acting on the world effectively. Center discussion around how we often focus on those things in our lives that are not working. Ask children to evaluate whether that really helps. Too often we learn to rely exclusively on what others perceive about us and put too little trust in introspection. If you can introduce children to the value of valuing themselves, you have truly presented those children with a gift they can keep forever.

CHOICES

Quality Necklaces: Invite children to cut strips of construction paper about five inches in length (provide as many colors as they want). Encourage children to write down one affirmation about themselves for each strip of paper. To make necklaces they should tape or staple one strip of paper together to make a small circle. Next, ask children to put the next strip of paper through this circle and tape or staple. Continue this process until they have enough circles to make a necklace. Encourage the children to wear their Quality Necklaces for all to see.

Quality Bands: Invite children to cut strips of construction paper big enough to wrap around their wrists. Ask children to put a positive message on the outside of their bands, decorate them, and wear them the rest of the day.

Quality Hats: Ask the children to design a hat using the hat pattern in the Resource Section. Ask them to cut out the pattern and to connect their hats with staples or tape. Encourage children to decorate their hats, write special or affirmative messages on them and wear their Quality Hats for all to see.

Quality Jewelry: Ask the children to create quality pins, quality earrings, quality rings, etc., all decorated with affirmations.

Quality Wardrobe: Ask children to tape pieces of colored construction paper with affirmations written on them to their wardrobe, transforming their clothes into quality shirts quality pants, quality shoes, etc. Encourage children to wear affirmations all day for all to see.

HAPPYWORK

Send a Family Gram home to explain the significance of self-affirmation and self-evaluation. Encourage family members to involve themselves with their children and to relate some of their accomplishments. Encourage children to record family affirmations in the Happy Journal and invite them to share with the group.

✎ **Notes**

The Thumbbodys

Purpose To learn that we are all unique and special in our own way

Materials Flip chart or blackboard, construction paper, ink pads

Time 20 minutes to make the Thumbbodys and 10 minutes to present and discuss

INSTRUCTIONS

Invite the children to think of all the people in their lives who they care about and who care about them. Make a list on a flip chart or blackboard for all to see.

Using ink pads and construction paper, ask children to use their thumbs to create prints on the paper in the shapes of Thumbbody people.

Ask the children to make their Thumbbodys represent themselves, their families, their friends, etc.

Ask children to title their pictures, "I Am Thumbbody Special."

DISCUSSION

This activity is an opportunity to teach children that we all have special qualities and talents. Present the concept of basic needs and how we choose to meet these needs in different ways. Children often believe that certain personality traits are more important or valuable than others. Focus on the children's strengths, discuss their own capabilities and how they are THUMBBODY special in their own ways.

CHOICES

The Thumbbody Buddies: The buddy system works well with this activity. Invite the children to choose a buddy, create their own personal Thumbbody, and share with each other the special qualities of their Thumbbody. Ask each child to share what they have learned about their buddy with the group.

Quality Stamps: Using an ink pad and positive stamps (you can obtain these in many school supply stores), encourage children to create messages about themselves on sheets of construction paper.

HAPPYWORK

Send home a Family Gram explaining the Thumbbody activity. Encourage children to interview family members to discover what they perceive as their qualities. Encourage the children to write down this information in their Happy Journals.

Smile Bingo

Purpose To introduce the value of self-evaluation

Materials Smile bingo cards, chips for cards, flip chart or blackboard

Time 45 minutes for game and discussion

INSTRUCTIONS

Invite children to challenge themselves to think of all their positive qualities. List these qualities on a flip chart or backboard for all to see.

Pass out Smile Bingo cards (see Resource Section) and play like regular bingo. Ask children to place a chip in the "smile" space if they believe they possess that special quality.

When a child obtains a Smile Bingo, invite them to read aloud the special qualities that are under the winning chips on their card. Encourage children to smile real big while their group member is reading aloud.

Note: You will need to run off two copies of the master Smile Bingo Cards. One copy can be cut up and then used to call numbers and positive traits. Use the other copy to keep track of the squares that have been played.

DISCUSSION

This activity helps children take a close look at successful behaviors. You may want to explain to your group members that if we choose successful behaviors, we can be happy. This is also a chance for children to recognize their worth. A variation is to have the children read their traits aloud from the bingo cards and then give examples of when they have used these behaviors. Also, present the concept of basic needs and how we all choose to meet these needs in different ways.

CHOICES

Games - Games - Games: Ask the children to tell a special quality about themselves before moving to the next chair, or base using such games as Musical Chairs, Duck-Duck Goose, Basketball, Baseball, or Relay Races. Use your imagination and have fun.

HAPPYWORK

Send home a Family Gram explaining the Smile Bingo activity. Encourage children to interview family members and discover what family members perceive their special qualities to be. Encourage them to write down this information in their Happy Journals. Invite them to share with their group members.

Musical Compliments

Purpose   To identify our strengths through positive affirmations

Materials   A ball (soft and safe), cassette player and tape, flip chart or blackboard

Time   15 minutes to play and discuss

INSTRUCTIONS

Ask group members to sit in a circle and to think of nice things about themselves or others. Make a list on a flip chart or blackboard for all to see.

Start the music and ask the children to pass the ball around the room to each other.

Stop the music and ask the child with the ball to say something nice or positive about themselves. You may want to ask a question to whomever has the ball and start the music after they answer.

Repeat this process several times.

DISCUSSION

This exercise helps children learn to meet their basic need for power. It focuses on their positive qualities and introduces children to self-recognition and evaluation. We recommend that you participate with the children.

CHOICES

If you would like the emphasis to be on the basic need for belonging as well as power, ask a child to throw the ball to a buddy and say something positive about that child.

Having A Ball: You can use this activity as a "get to know one another" activity much like the Toilet Paper Game. Ask the children to pass the ball around, and when the music stops, invite them to share with the group one thing about themselves that other group members would not know unless they told them.

Quality Musical Chairs: This game is played the same way as traditional musical chairs. Place an affirmation under each chair, such as I'm helpful, I'm smart, I'm wonderful, etc. Have one less number of chairs as there are participants. Play music and when you stop the music, instruct each child to sit in a chair. Ask each child who got a seat to read their affirmation out loud. Ask the child who did not get a seat to say something affirming about themselves and to leave the circle. Take one chair away and start the music.

HAPPYWORK

Send a Family Gram home to explain the significance of self-affirmation and self-evaluation. Encourage family members to relate some of their accomplishments. Encourage the children to record family accomplishments in the Happy Journal and invite them to share with the group.

✎ **Notes**

Do Like - Don't Like Collage

Purpose To learn about our own and other group members' unique perceptions

Materials Magazines, scissors, glue, construction paper, markers

Time 45 minutes to make, present, and discuss collages

INSTRUCTIONS

On a flip chart or backboard, make two columns. Designate one DO LIKE and the other DON'T LIKE.

Ask children to think of all the qualities they like and don't like about themselves and others. Write them on a chart.

Ask children to describe what they perceive individuals to "look" like who exhibit each of these DO LIKE and DON'T LIKE qualities.

Give each child two sheets of construction paper and ask them to label them DO LIKE and DON'T LIKE.

Encourage children to look through magazines and cut out pictures of people they perceive they would like to get to know and those from who they would want to stay away. Ask them to paste these pictures on the construction paper creating a collage.

Invite children to share both collages with their group members.

DISCUSSION

This is an imaginative activity that introduces being conscious of their perceptions. Emphasize this concept when the children have different pictures of how these DO LIKES and DON'T LIKES look. Ask children how they perceive themselves and ask them to illustrate this by finding pictures in the magazine that "look" like them. Present the concept of our basic needs and how we all choose to meet these basic needs in different ways. Children often believe that certain personality traits are more important or valuable than others. Focusing on the children's strengths may be an opportunity to discuss their own capabilities and how they are special in their own way.

CHOICES

To streamline this activity, ask children to cut out two pictures from a magazine, one representing a DO LIKE image and the other a DON'T LIKE image. Invite children to share the pictures with the group and to tell the group what it is about the pictures they like and dislike.

HAPPYWORK

Send home a Family Gram to clarify the intention of the DO LIKE - DON'T LIKE Collage activity and explain the idea of perceptions. Encourage children to interview family members and discover what family members like and don't like about others. Encourage parents to find pictures people in magazines and talk to their children about what they perceive about them. Encourage children to write down this information in their Happy Journal and share with their group members.

 Notes

Quality Clothespins

Purpose   To recognize our effective behaviors and positive qualities

Materials   Flip chart or blackboard, heavy construction paper, boy and girl patterns, clothespins, markers, crayons, yarn, and small slips of paper entitled "Quality Notes"

Time   45 minutes to create, present, and discuss Quality Clothespins

INSTRUCTIONS

Invite children to come together and brainstorm affirmations about themselves. List the statements on a flip chart or a blackboard for all to see.

Give each child one pre-cut boy or girl pattern (see the Resource Section). Ask them to write their names, color, and draw on them to resemble themselves.

Ask them to glue a clothespin to the back of their character and hang it in the room on a clothesline made from yarn or heavy string.

Encourage children to write at least three positive qualities about themselves on the Quality Notes. Ask them to attach their "quality notes" to their clothespins and display for all to see.

Ask a buddy or other group members to add one "quality note" to each group member's clothespin.

Encourage children to add Quality Notes to their clothespins routinely.

DISCUSSION

Often the way we choose to perceive ourselves is the way we will be perceived by others. This activity is useful in encouraging children to look at what they are doing and how they are already acting on the world effectively. Center discussion around how we often focus on those things in our lives that are not working. Ask children to ask themselves whether or not that really helps. Further, at an early age we learn to whom we look for our feedback. Too often we learn to rely exclusively on what others perceive about us and trust little on introspection. If you can introduce a child to the value of valuing yourself, you have truly presented that child with a gift they can keep forever.

CHOICES

Let's "FACE" it — I AM GREAT!: Ask each child to cut a large circle out of construction paper and draw their face. Follow by asking each child to write at least three special qualities about themselves on their face. Encourage children to pass their face around to other group members. Ask children to add one special quality to other group members' "faces." When finished, invite each child to FACE IT and share their qualities with the group.

HAPPYWORK

Send a Family Gram home to explain to the family the significance of self-affirmation and self-evaluation. Encourage family members to involve themselves with their children and to relate some of their accomplishments. Encourage children to record family affirmations in the Happy Journals and invite them to share with the group.

✎ **Notes**

Star Search

Purpose   To recognize and identify our special talents

Materials   Colored construction paper, star pattern, tinfoil, glue, scissors, markers

Time   35 minutes for brainstorming, making stars, and performing

INSTRUCTIONS

Tell children that you are conducting a Star Search and are looking for stars.

Encourage children to share what they do well with their group members and make a list for all to see. Ask other group members to think of other things their group members do well and add them to the list. Examples could be sing, dance, turn a flip, recite poetry, get good grades, hit a baseball, etc.

After you have listed each child's talents, ask them to choose one that they can perform for the Star Search. If the talent can't be demonstrated in front of the group, they can talk about their accomplishments.

We recommend that you choose a talent and take your turn.

Following each child's star presentation, encourage group members to clap and yell as loud as they can.

After all the children have performed, ask them to make tin foil stars (see Resource Section) and draw a picture of themselves to paste in the center of the stars. Ask them to put their name and the talent they demonstrated on their stars. Hang them in the room like real stars for all to see.

DISCUSSION

This activity is an opportunity to acquaint children with the idea that we all have special qualities and talents. (Children often believe that certain talents are more important or valuable than others.) You may want to challenge children to think of other talents they know people have. Present the concept of our basic need for power or worth and how we all choose to meet this need in different ways. This activity can be used to introduce a discussion on whether certain capabilities are better than others and to emphasize the significance of doing the best one can.

CHOICES

If time is a factor, simply identify a talent, create the stars, and display them.
If possible, use a Polaroid shot to place in the center of each tin foil star.

Constellation Search: Ask the group to challenge themselves to perform a group talent. This may work well with the Cheers activity in this workbook. Another choice may be to coordinate a group project such as a bake sale, car wash, community clean up, etc. Make one big star and place a group picture in the center. Use the analogy of how special stars in the universe work together to form constellations. Performing together as a group further introduces group members to the basic needs for belonging and power.

HAPPYWORK

Send home a Family Gram clarifying to parents the intention of the Star Search activity. Encourage children to interview family members and discover what they believe are their talents. Encourage children to make a personalized star and award it to a family member.

✎ <u>Notes</u>

Read All About It!

Purpose   To look into our quality worlds to see who we want to become

Materials   Construction paper, note paper, pens, paste, magazines

Time   10 minutes to write each story and 45 minutes to design newspapers

INSTRUCTIONS

Invite each child to write newspaper articles about themselves. If the children are too young to write, have them tell you their stories and you can write them.

Depending on what you want the focus of the newspaper to be, ask children to report on the following:

- significant events in which they are currently involved
- successful events from their past
- famous things they will do in the future
- accomplishments of the group
- something of merit the group plans to do in the future

Encourage children to give their articles a headline just like the front page of a newspaper.

Invite the children to help you organize the articles and glue them on construction paper. Name your newspaper, paste phrases and pictures from magazines, illustrate, then "take to print" by making photocopies. Pass out plenty of newspapers for the children to take home to give to their friends.

DISCUSSION

Use those articles that represent who they will be in the future to help children discuss what they need to do to accomplish their dreams. If the wishes seem out of reach or extreme, ask them these questions:

- If you reached your dream, what would you have then that you don't have now? (Relate it to the basic needs, LOVE, POWER, FREEDOM, FUN.)

- Are there any choices that you can make that will help you get some of what you really want?

This is also an opportunity to discuss the value of setting goals and how to reach those goals.

CHOICES

Quality Interview: Combine this activity with the Quality Interview activity in this workbook. Not only would the interview help children learn what it takes to reach their goals, but interviews could be put in the newspapers.

Commercial About Me: Ask children to use a tape recorder and blank tape to make a commercial about themselves. The purpose of the commercial is for the children to market themselves as wonderful friends for other children. Ask them to include positive statements about their personality, interests, looks, skills, etc. The commercial could also focus on those goals they have for their futures. Group members could do a group commercial, all taking turns selling their group as a "quality group." (Time: 10 minutes per commercial)

HAPPYWORK

Ask children to write an article about something significant that a family member or the entire family has accomplished. The article could also focus on an upcoming event such as a trip, someone graduating, an anticipated baby, etc. (These articles could also be used for a newspaper or scrapbook.) We recommend that you send home a Family Gram to help family members understand the purpose of the assignment.

✎ **Notes**

Affirmation of Others

Balloon Game

Purpose   To invite children to identify the strengths of each group member

Materials   Balloons in several colors, markers, flip chart or blackboard

Time   5 minutes to make balloons, 15 minutes for play and discussion

INSTRUCTIONS

Ask group members to sit in a circle and to challenge themselves to think of all the nice things they could say about someone else. Make a list on a flip chart or blackboard for all to see.

Encourage each child to pick a balloon from the several colors available. (Choices are important.)

Ask the children to draw their faces on the balloons and to write their name on them.

Invite the children to bat the balloons around until you say "stop." At this time, ask each child to grab a balloon and offer a compliment to whomever's balloon they are holding.

If the children get their own balloons, ask them to come to you or their buddy and tell something positive about themselves.

Repeat this process several times.

DISCUSSION

This exercise, like others presented in Section C, help children learn about the value of others. Control Theory demonstrates that we are the same but our needs and wants make us different. We have found it beneficial to help children to understand these concepts through recognizing the positive traits of others. Ask the children how they feel when they affirm others.

CHOICES

Musical Balloons: As with the Musical Compliments activity, play music as the children bat around the balloons. Ask them to catch a balloon when the music stops and offer positive feedback to the owner of the balloon they are holding. Start the music and repeat several times.

Buddy Balloons: Ask each child to pick a buddy. Ask them to bat one of their balloons back and forth. When one buddy catches the balloon, ask them to give a compliment to their partner. When the balloon comes back to its owner, ask the owner to give a compliment to themself. After a few minutes, ask them to use the other person's balloon and repeat the process.

As with the Let's Face It activity, encourage children to write compliments on the balloons. Invite children to share their balloons with the group, reading their affirmations aloud.

HAPPYWORK

Encourage children to make a balloon for a family member. Ask them to write all the compliments they can think of about that person on their balloon and give it the person. Send home a Family Gram to help family members understand the intention of The Balloon Game.

Notes

Giant Pictures

Purpose   To discover the value of recognizing our positive qualities

Materials   Large sheets of bulletin board paper or table cloths, pencils, crayons, magic markers, scissors

Time   20 minutes for drawing, 5 minutes for presenting each child's picture

INSTRUCTIONS

Ask group members to sit in a circle and challenge themselves to think of nice things about their group members. Suggestions could be smart, athletic, pretty smile, fun, helps others, etc. Make a list on a chart or blackboard for all to see.

Ask a child to lie down on a large sheet of bulletin board paper while you or another child trace their body.

Ask the child who has been traced to put their name in big letters on the paper.

Encourage the children to take turns offering positive qualities about that person using the suggestions on the flip chart. Write down the suggestions inside of the traced figure. Ask each child to hang their Giant Picture up on the wall for all to see.

DISCUSSION

This exercise introduces children to traits that are positive and demonstrate worth. Not only will children recognize worthy traits within themselves, but they will also have the opportunity to learn what is praiseworthy about others. Children may have been exposed to attitudes that devalue others. By giving them the opportunity to see the value of others, they may have new information they can act on in the future.

CHOICES

Giant Groups: After all the individual Giant Pictures are traced and the positive qualities have been added to each picture, tape all the pictures together and discuss with the children how quality individuals can connect to become a quality group.

If you want the emphasis of this exercise to be on belonging rather than self-worth, get a sheet of paper large enough to trace everyone at one time. Ask children to brainstorm for positive qualities of their group. List these qualities on the large group illustration and hang it in the room for all to see.

HAPPYWORK

Ask each child to choose a family member and list the positive qualities they recognize about that person in their Happy Journal. Let each child share their Happywork assignment with their group members if they choose to do so. Remember to send home a Family Gram to help parents appreciate the value of recognizing the worth of others.

✎ Notes

Pats On The Back

Purpose To give fellow group members encouragement

Materials Flip chart or blackboard, construction paper, markers, scissors, tape

Time 45 minutes for activity and discussion

INSTRUCTIONS

Ask group members to sit in a circle and think of Pats On The Back, or nice things, they can say to their group members. Make a list on a flip chart or blackboard.

Ask children to trace their hands on construction paper, cut them out, and write their names on them.

Encourage children to choose a buddy and exchange their cut-out hands. Ask each buddy to write positive affirmations about each other on the hands. Invite the children to tape their "hands" on their backs and wear them for all to see. Don't forget your own Pat On The Back!

DISCUSSION

Control Theory explains that our perceptions are defined by our experiences and that our view of the world is influenced in our formative years. Control Theory also says that we can add new perceptions. As children understand their values and others' values, they learn valuable information that can help them empower themselves. Pats On The Back helps children add the perception that others have value.

CHOICES

Super Hero Capes: Invite children to make super hero capes using long sheets of construction paper, markers, and yarn. Tape the capes to the clothes on their backs. Encourage group members to write positive messages to other children on their capes. Encourage children to go "trick or treating" for compliments for the rest of the day. Ask children to read what is written on their capes to the group members.

Mailbox Game: Encourage the children to place compliments, positive sayings, and affirmations in another child's mailbox.

HAPPYWORK

Encourage children to make a super hero cape for a family member. Ask them to write compliments about that person on the cape and give it to the family member. Send home a Family Gram to help family members understand the Pat On The Back activity.

Mailbox Game

Purpose   To give positive feedback to group members

Materials   Strips of paper, pencils, shoes, blackboard or flip chart

Time   15 minutes to stuff mailboxes, 15 minutes to read and discuss mail

INSTRUCTIONS

Encourage group members to sit in a circle and to challenge themselves to think of all the nice things they could say about someone else. Make a list on a flip chart or blackboard for all to see.

Ask each child to take one shoe off, place it in the middle of the circle, and pretend that the shoes are their Mailboxes.

Give each child enough strips of paper so they have one for each member of their group.

Ask them to write one positive statement for each of their group members on the strips of paper and put them in their Mailboxes.

After everyone is finished distributing the mail, ask group members to read their mail aloud.

DISCUSSION

This exercise helps children understand the value of themselves and others. As with the Balloon Game, Giant Pictures, and Pats On The Back, the Mailbox Game helps expand their perceptual system to include messages that say, "I am special." You may want to present the basic needs as part of this exercise and ask the children what needs they met with positive affirmations. Helping others understand their worth can help children meet the need for power. This can be a valuable tool to help children relate to others as they reach adulthood.

CHOICES

Buddy Box: Encourage children to choose a buddy and make a buddy box out of a shoe box or a cigar box. Ask children to put their names on the mailboxes and to keep them for permanent use during group or class. You may want to designate a space for all the buddy boxes to go. Ask children to place a positive note in the buddy box each day.

Group Box: Make a group mailbox and encourage children to write positive notes to one another each day.

Autograph Books: Make a book out of construction paper (see Happy Book Activity). Encourage children to write in each other's books at the end of each group session. Encourage children to take the books home for their family to see.

You may want to combine this activity with the Happy Letters activity.

HAPPYWORK

Ask each child to make a list of positive statements about a family member, write them on strips of paper, insert in envelopes (optional), and place the envelops in their mailbox at home for that special person. Send home a Family Gram to help family members understand the intention of the Mailbox Game activity.

 Notes

Happy Letters

Purpose   To write positive, need-fulfilling letters to group members

Materials   Writing paper, pencils, envelopes, stamps

Time   45 minutes to write letters

INSTRUCTIONS

Invite group members to sit in a circle and to challenge themselves to think of all the nice things they could say about others in their group. List on a flip chart or blackboard for all to see.

Ask each child to write their full name and mailing address on an envelope and put the envelope face down in a large box.

Invite children to draw an envelope from the box and to keep the name on the envelope secret.

Ask each child to write a letter to the group member they have chosen focusing on the positive traits of that person. Remind children to refer to the list of positive things on the master list that the group made.

We recommend that you ask the children to share their letters with you. Help the children stuff, seal, and stamp the envelopes.

Take a walk to a nearby mailbox or make a mailbox so the children can mail their Happy Letters.

DISCUSSION

Everyone likes getting mail and reading about themselves through the eyes of others. Be sure you have discussions about what is effective to write one another. Happy Letters are a tool for helping children to focus on and then record what they value about their group members. Store their Happy Letters in a personal folder to help group members develop a success identity.

CHOICES

Pen Pals: Group members can write letters to all the members in the group or choose a secret buddy for whom to write letters on an ongoing basis.

Invite children to write a letter to themselves and send it in the mail to themselves.

HAPPYWORK

Ask group members to write and send a Happy Letter to someone in their family. Send home a Family Gram to help family members understand the purpose of the Happy Letter activity.

✎ **Notes**

Need-Fulfilling Ornaments

Purpose   To explore why giving to others is need-fulfilling

Materials   Recipe: 4 cups of flour, 1 cup of salt, 1 1/2 cups of water, cookie cutters, buttons, sequins, beads, ribbon, shellac

Time   1 hour to bake ornaments and 45 minutes to decorate, present, and discuss

INSTRUCTIONS

Invite children to help mix the dough and cut out the ornaments. Poke a hole at the top of the ornaments before baking. (Ornaments may be pre-baked.)

Bake at 200 degrees for one hour. Once they have cooled, paint, decorate, and apply shellac to the ornaments. Put a piece of ribbon through the hole in each ornament so it can be hung or worn as a necklace.

Ask children to share what they have made with the group and ask them to tell to whom they choose to give their gift.

Some questions you may want to ask are:

- How does it feel to give to others?
- How do others feel when they receive gifts?
- Why do you think giving and receiving feels good?

DISCUSSION

This exercise is an opportunity for you to discuss the need-fulfilling aspect of giving to others. Suggest that one reason is that both the giver and receiver are getting most of their basic needs met at the same time. You can introduce the basic needs by asking:

Was it need-fulfilling to make something of which they were proud (power)?
Was it fun?
Were they creative and did they have a lot of choices (freedom)?
Could they share their ornament with someone they care about (love)?
Is it need-fulfilling for the recipient?
Does the recipient feel important when they accept the gift?

We recommend that you ask children to make something and give it to themselves. Discuss how it is need-fulfilling to give yourself a gift.

CHOICES

Special Coupons: Encourage children to think of gifts that they could give to someone else that would cost little money and still mean a lot to the other person. List suggestions on a flip chart or black board for all to see. Some examples of ideas could be coupons for hugs, for a free car wash, for helping out around the house, for one hassle-free homework night, etc. Ask each child to choose one or two of these ideas and write them on a small piece of paper and make their special coupon. Ask children to place coupons in envelopes, decorate the envelopes anyway they choose, and present them to the lucky recipient. (Time: 45 minutes for activity and discussion)

HAPPYWORK

Ask children to write in their Happy Journal what they were thinking and feeling when they gave their gift or when they helped their special someone. Send a Family Gram to let parents know about the purpose of this activity.

Notes

The Helping Game

Purpose To explore why helping others is need-fulfilling

Materials Small cards with pictures or words describing situations which require help from a friend

Time 45 minutes for activity

INSTRUCTIONS

Separate students into two teams. Ask for two volunteers, one child from each group.

Ask volunteer #1 to pick one of the small index cards provided and act out the problem listed on the card. (See Resource Section.)

Invite volunteer #2 to come up with some ideas of how they could help.

Encourage ideas from the rest of the group members. Ask group members to cheer if they think the HELPING suggestions are suitable.

Repeat several times.

DISCUSSION

This exercise is an opportunity for you to discuss with children why helping others is need-fulfilling. You can introduce the basic needs by asking if it is need-fulfilling for the person who was helping. For example, did they feel important (power) and did they feel caring about the other person (love). You can further introduce that it is need-fulfilling for the recipient because they see themselves as important when accepting the help and they feel love and belonging when accepting help from someone they care about. Ask children if they can think of something they can do to help themselves.

CHOICES

Helping Hands: On colored pieces of construction paper, ask children to trace their hands and cut them out. On the palm of the hand, ask children to print their name and write "Helping Hand". Ask each child to write on each finger ways they can be "Helping Hands" to their family, group members, teachers, etc. Each hand and their fingers could be used to represent a specific person to be helped and the ways the child might help that person. Ask children to choose one of the ways they have identified and act on it. Invite them to evaluate their choice with the group. (Time: 45 minutes for activity and discussion)

Role Play: In smaller groups ask the children to role play a problem while others brainstorm how to help. Encourage each child in the group to suggest a solution to the problem. After each suggestion has been heard, ask the child who presented the problem to choose a plan.

The Giving Tree: Invite children to make apples using construction paper to hang on a tree. Ask children to write GIVING statements on the apples such as:

- Help someone with their homework.
- Help the group leader clean up after the meeting.
- Recognize someone for something nice they did today.

Invite children to pick "an apple a day" and to follow through with the request that is written on the apple. Ask children to put their apples back on the tree when they are finished so another group member can pick it the next time.

HAPPYWORK

Ask children to think of something they could do for someone at home, for example, helping with a problem or helping with a task. Invite them to brainstorm with the group about what they can do to help and encourage them to follow through with their plan at home. Send home a Family Gram to clarify to family members the purpose of this project.

✎ **Notes**

Learning About Oneself and Others

Quality Star Puzzle

Purpose   To introduce the five basic needs (survival, love, power fun, freedom) and the pictures we choose to satisfy our needs

Materials   Pre-cut construction paper star puzzles, scissors, glue, construction paper in several colors, markers

Time   20 minutes for creating stars, 10 minutes for discussing needs

INSTRUCTIONS

Give each child the pieces to their Quality Star Puzzle (see Resource section) and ask them to choose a sheet of construction paper from the different colors available. (Choices are important.)

Ask each child to put their name on the piece of construction paper and write or draw an answer to the following five questions on the five puzzle pieces.

- What is one thing you choose to do for fun?
- What is one thing that you do well?
- Who is one person who thinks you are special?
- Where is a special place that you can choose to go?
- What is one way you choose to be healthy?

After the children have answered all five questions, encourage each child to put together their Quality Star Puzzle and glue it on the construction paper.

Invite each child to share their Quality Star with the group members. Hang all stars around the room to resemble stars in the sky.

DISCUSSION

The basic needs work very closely together just like the points of a star. Offer the analogy that all points of a star must shine to make it a true star. Similarly, we must also choose ways to meet all of our needs so we can shine. Encourage children to help their group members think of answers to the five questions. Point out that, although we are different, we are all "star attractions" in our own special way.

CHOICES

High Five: Invite group members to trace their hands on a piece of construction paper and to share their drawing with a designated buddy. Ask children the five questions concerning their basic needs and encourage them to write the answers on the fingers of their traced hand. Offer the analogy that we all need our five fingers so our hands will be effective. Similarly, we must choose ways to meet all five of our needs so we can be effective. After the discussion, encourage group members to share what they found out about themselves with their buddies and give their new friend a "high five."

85

Quality Circle: Invite group members to choose a buddy. Ask children the five questions concerning their basic needs and encourage them to put their answers in the inside segments of their Quality Circles (see Resource Section.) Ask the children to add other ways they could satisfy their basic needs on the outside of the circles. Encourage children to share with their buddies and other group members.

To encourage group cohesiveness, make one big Quality Star Puzzle or one big Quality Circle. Encourage all group members to answer all five questions together. Fill in each segment with all the answers.

HAPPYWORK

Encourage children to take home a Quality Star Puzzle, Quality Circle, or High Five and present it to a family member. Remember to send home a Family Gram explaining the purpose of this activity.

Notes

Pictures Ablowing

Purpose To understand that we have the same basic needs and we have unique pictures of how to meet our needs

Materials Large room, chairs, small strips of paper with written directions

Time 15 minutes for game and 10 minutes for discussion

INSTRUCTIONS

Arrange chairs in a circle (one less than number of participants). Recruit a volunteer and ask them to stand in the middle of the circle. Encourage all other children to choose a seat.

On a piece of paper write several statements that describe different interests, personality traits, etc. and put them in a bag. Examples of statements could be:

- Everyone who likes to play softball
- Everyone who can turn a cartwheel
- Everyone who can ride a bike
- Everyone who made a good choice today
- Everyone who is proud of something they did today

Ask the child in the middle to choose a piece of paper, read the printed statement, then yell "Pictures Ablowing."

At this time, ask children who believe that the statement applies to them to get up and go to another empty chair. The child in the middle also goes for one of the empty chairs. Ask the children who moved, what basic need this particular statement satisfied.

Ask the child who is left standing in the center to read the next piece of paper. Repeat as many times as you want.

DISCUSSION

This is an effective activity to demonstrate to children that we all have similarities and differences but that also we are all basically the same. Explain to children that we are all special and that it is our pictures that make us unique. At this time you may want to discuss the importance of accepting others and their differences.

CHOICES

Instead of using chairs, have children stand up from their seats. Ask children to take turns reading the statements.

Ask children to think of their own statements.

HAPPYWORK

Ask children to choose a family member and make a list in their Happy Journal of those things that are the same about them and those things that are different. We recommend that you send home a list of questions in a Family Gram. Encourage children to share their lists with the group.

✎ **Notes**

Which Are You?

Purpose   To understand that often we have to choose from more than one picture to satisfy a basic need

Materials   Large room

Time   20 minutes for activity and discussion

INSTRUCTIONS

Ask children to stand in the center of the room.
Say to children, "WHICH ARE YOU, _____ or _____?"
Some examples of choices are:

- Vanilla or Chocolate
- Mountains or Beaches
- Football or Basketball
- Ninja Turtles or Transformers
- Rock or Rap
- Spelling or Math
- Dogs or Cats (etc.)

Point to the side of the room (left or right) that you want children to go after they make their choice. Tell them they must choose one or the other.

After they moved to their side of the room, encourage them to notice who is there with them and who is not. Ask them to come back to the center and present another choice.

DISCUSSION

This is an effective activity to demonstrate similarities and differences. Explain to the children that we are all special and that it is our pictures that make us unique. Some children will have difficulty in choosing. You may want to take the opportunity to discuss that sometimes we have several pictures in our quality worlds such as two things that we really value or want. It is these pictures that causes confusion or conflict. Sometimes, in the case of two conflicting pictures or wants, we have to choose.

CHOICES

After each choice, ask children to pick a buddy on the other side of the room and encourage them to share why they made their choice.

HAPPYWORK

Encourage children to choose a family member, preferably a parent, and ask that person if they have ever had to make a difficult choice. Invite the child to write about what their family member said in their Happy Journal and to share it with their group members. Remember to send home a Family Gram to help family members understand the purpose of this activity and how they can best help their child.

(The Which Are You? activity was conceived and revised from *Values Clarification*, Simon, Howe, and Klrschenbaum, Values Associates 1978)

Notes

Me Collage

Purpose   To identify our strengths through pictures and words

Materials   Magazines, large sheets of construction paper, scissors, glue, magic markers

Time   45 minutes to construct, present, and discuss collages

INSTRUCTIONS

Ask each child to draw a picture of themselves in the middle of a large sheet of construction paper.

Ask each child to cut out and paste pictures, words, and phrases from magazines which describe ways that they picture themselves.

Make your own Me Collage and share it with the group.

DISCUSSION

This is an opportunity to confirm that each of the pictures the children chose for their collages satisfy one or more basic needs in their quality worlds. When introducing this activity, we recommend that you participate with the children, and make your own Me Collage. Be enthusiastic over the qualities you chose to recognize about yourself.

CHOICES

Like Me - Not Like Me Collage: Ask each child to look through magazines and find pictures which represent things that are "like them" and that "are not like them."

Group Collage: If you would like the emphasis of the activity to be on belonging as well as power, ask children to draw a picture of their group on a large piece of poster board and cut out pictures or phrases which describe things that the group likes to do.

Me Bag: Ask children to draw a picture of themselves in the middle of a paper bag and decorate the bag anyway they want. Encourage children to cut out pictures from magazines or collect items that represent themselves and fill their bags with these items. Invite each child to present their bag to the group members.

Take Polaroid shots of each child or of the entire group or ask them to bring a picture of themselves from home. Use the pictures for the center of the collages or put them on the Me Bag.

HAPPYWORK

The Me Collage could also be a Family Collage. Ask children to follow the same instructions, replacing pictures and phrases about themselves with those that represent their family. Send home a Family Gram to encourage family members to take part in this activity.

✎ **Notes**

Happy Mobiles

Purpose   To creatively express activities, people, things, and choices that truly make us happy

Materials   Clothes hangers, yarn, scissors, construction paper in several colors, hole puncher, markers, patterns of mobile shapes

Time   35 minutes to make mobiles, 5 minutes to present and discuss

INSTRUCTIONS

Ask the children to cut out different shapes, all about the same size, from different colors of construction paper.

Ask group members to punch a hole in the top of each shape, tie yarn through the holes, and write their name on one of the shapes.

On the other shapes, encourage children to draw about or write down the things, people, and choices that make them happy.

When they are finished, ask the children to attach the yarn to a clothes hanger and hang for all to see.

DISCUSSION

This is an opportunity for group members to learn about themselves and about each other. If children have trouble thinking of what makes them happy use the buddy system or have other group members help them come up with ideas. This exercise introduces to group members that even though we all have the same basic needs, we still are unique and special.

CHOICES

What I Do Well Mobile: Ask each child to write down or draw one thing they do well or positive phrases about themselves on each shape.

People I Love Mobile: Ask each child to write or draw people they love and people that love them on each slip. These cut-outs could be heart shaped.

I Am Fun Mobile: Ask each child to write or draw what they do for fun. This mobile could have funny shapes and children could choose to write with glitter.

I Have Choices Mobile: Ask each child to write or draw choices they make in their daily life.

We Are A Happy Group Mobile: Ask group members to make a group mobile and write ways they are successful as a group on the mobile shapes.

HAPPYWORK

Send home a Family Gram and encourage family members to participate in making a Family Mobile. Ask children to take blank mobiles home and ask family members to complete them.

✎ <u>Notes</u>

Paper Bag Puppets

Purpose   To talk about ourselves and learn about each other

Materials   Paper bags, construction paper, yarn, markers, glue, scraps of materials, buttons, and decorative materials

Time   20 minutes to make puppets, 3 minutes for presentation

INSTRUCTIONS

Ask children to make a puppet that represents themselves using paper bags and decorative materials.

Ask each child to have the puppets tell their group about:

- Things they do well
- Activities they choose to do for fun
- Choices they make that are good
- Things they choose to do to take care of their physical selves
- People they love and people that love them

DISCUSSION

It is important to make your own puppet. Introduce this activity with an explanation of the basic needs. Discuss that, although we all have the same needs, we choose to act on them in different ways. Explain that these differences make us special.

CHOICES

Puppet Stage: Children could construct a puppet stage using a refrigerator box with a hole cut out or a table with a curtain in front.

Puppets As A Therapeutic Tool: Puppets are an impressive medium for helping children communicate with you, one another, or with themselves. Any of the activities presented in this workbook could be dramatized with the use of puppets. If children are not opening up in the group setting, we highly recommend that you explore puppetry as a therapeutic tool. (See the Power of Puppets in the Process Section.)

HAPPYWORK

Ask the children to write in their Happy Journals one way they satisfy their basic needs each day. Send home a Family Gram to explain how family members can help children understand these concepts. Encourage children to show their Happy Journals to their parents.

Cookie Bears

Purpose To learn that we are all unique because of the choices we make

Materials Small toaster oven, cookie dough, bear cookie cutter, candy sprinkles, M & M's, and other edible decorations

Time 10 minutes to plan party (on the previous day), 45 minutes to make, decorate, and present cookies

INSTRUCTIONS

Plan a cookie party with your group. Ask children to bring decorations from home. Invite each child to help prepare for the party and to help with making the cookie dough. Ask each child to cut out bears, place them on a cookie sheet, and bake.

After your discussion (below), ask the children to decorate the bear cookies and give them the opportunity to show their bears to the group.

DISCUSSION

While the cookies are baking, introduce the children to the concept that we all have the same basic needs. Continue by explaining that we do, however, add things to our lives as we grow that "decorate" our lives or make each of us special. While the children are decorating their cookies, ask them what things they have chosen in their lives that "decorate" them. Invite the children to share with the group.

CHOICES

Use other cookie cutter shapes or ask the children to shape dough into people, or toast bread and decorate with peanut butter, jelly, bananas or fruit.

HAPPYWORK

Ask children to add one "decoration" to their lives this week and write it down in their Happy Journals. Send home a Family Gram to encourage the family's participation.

✎ Notes

Happy Books

Purpose To create a narrative that helps us understand what makes us happy

Materials Construction paper in several colors, hole puncher, scissors, yarn, markers, crayons

Time 30 minutes to make books, 15 minutes to present and discuss

INSTRUCTIONS

Ask the children to punch holes through several pieces of colored construction paper and connect the pages with yarn to make Happy Books. Ask them to write their names and decorate the covers of their books.

Invite children to write or draw in their Happy Books about the theme presented in the group that day. A library of Happy Books could evolve by using the ideas in the Choices Section.

We recommend that you design your own Happy Book and present it to your group.

DISCUSSION

This activity helps group members learn about themselves and about each other. If children cannot think of things to put in their Happy Books use the buddy system or have other group members brainstorm ideas. Explain that we are unique and we all have lives worthy of a Happy Book.

CHOICES

What I Do Well Book: Invite each child to write down or draw one thing they do well on each page.

People I Love Book: Ask each child to write down or draw people they love and people that love them. This book could be heart shaped.

I Am Fun Book: Ask each child to write or draw things they do for fun. This book could be in "funny shapes" or children could choose to write or draw with glitter.

I Have Choices Book: Ask each child to write down or draw the effective choices that they make in their daily lives.

I Am Successful Book: Ask children to think of a problem they are having and write down or draw a story that shows them working it out.

We Are A Happy Group Book: Ask group members to make a group book in which they write ways they are successful as a group.

HAPPYWORK

If family involvement is strong, suggest a "We Are a Happy Family Book". Encourage children to take blank books home and ask family members to fill in the pages. Don't forget to send home a Family Gram.

✎ Notes

Feeling, Thinking, and Doing Behaviors

Flush That Stinkin' Thinkin'

Purpose To learn that we can control how we choose to think

Materials Rolls of toilet paper, markers, functioning toilet, flip chart or blackboard

Time 20 minutes to list, discuss, and flush negative thoughts

INSTRUCTIONS

Discuss the importance of thinking positive thoughts with the children and that they have a choice of what to think.

Ask children to write on squares of toilet paper any negative words they use to describe themselves or others. For examples ugly, stupid, nerd, etc.

Ask the group to participate with you in a ceremonial flushing of all their Stinkin' Thinkin'.

Encourage children to help you make a list of positive, happy, complementary thoughts. Display for all to see.

DISCUSSION

This is a great exercise to do before several of the activities that promote practicing positive affirmations of self and others. Children can learn at an early age that they have control over what they think and can choose to act on those positive thoughts. You may want to challenge children to think of ways to help them steer away from negative thoughts. An example would be for children to choose to play with children who are positive and don't choose Stinkin' Thinkin'.

CHOICES

Trash that stinkin' thinkin': Instead of using toilet paper, use notebook paper and ask children to throw the negative words in a trash can.

Ask children to list their own positive thoughts on note book paper or in their Happy Journals and to read them aloud.

HAPPYWORK

Ask children to challenge themselves to remember every time they begin to choose Stinkin' Thinkin'. Ask them to write the Stinkin' Thinkin' word in their Happy Journal and put a big **X** over it. Then ask them to list a positive thought or a compliment about themselves. Give them the option of sharing their Happy Journal with the group members. Send home a Family Gram and encourage parents to help children recognize Stinkin' Thinkin' and remind them to do their Happywork.

Happy Sad Collage

Purpose   To introduce the concept of positive and negative signals

Materials   Magazines, construction paper, scissors, glue, magic markers, crayons

Time   35 minutes to make and present collage, 15 minutes to discuss signals

INSTRUCTIONS

Ask the children to look in magazines for pictures, phrases, or words that make them feel good when they look at them. Ask them to think about how they know that the pictures make them happy. Ask them to cut out the pictures and glue them on a large sheet of construction paper.

After this is completed, ask them to write down activities, people, or things on their collage that feel good when they think about them, such as playing games, helping others, watching movies, etc. On another day, or if time permits, ask them to do the same for those things that feel bad.

Talk to the group about their pictures. You may want to ask questions such as:

- What are signals? What signals do you get?
- What is it about each picture that feels good or bad?
- How do you know when you feel good or bad?
- What choices do you have when you get a positive (happy)
   or negative (sad) signal?

DISCUSSION

Children as young as three or four years old can begin to recognize and understand their signals. They can also begin to learn that they have a choice once they feel a signal. Positive signals are important to recognize so we can begin to understand what choices we have to help make us happy. Negative signals are important to explore so we can begin to learn and act on those behaviors that hurt us.

CHOICES

Ask one group to make a Happy Collage and one to make a Sad Collage. Encourage children to share and discuss their collages.

Ask children to act out some things that feel good or that feel bad. Remember to explore choices.

Happy Face - Sad Face Collage: Invite children to draw a happy or sad face in the middle of a large sheet of poster board. Encourage them to make their collages around each face.

HAPPYWORK

Send home a Family Gram to tell parents the purpose of this exercise. Ask children to write "happy" and "sad" on the top of two separate pages in their Happy Journals. Encourage them to write down each day what they were doing when they recognized a positive or a negative signal. Ask children to share with the group.

✎ **Notes**

Alligator River

Purpose To learn that thinking positively is something we control and can choose to do

Materials Colored construction paper, hour glass, large room

Time 10 minutes to cut out rocks, 45 minutes to play and discuss game

INSTRUCTIONS

Divide group members into two teams and ask them to think of all the nice things they can say about themselves or about individuals in their group. Make a list on a flip chart or blackboard for all to see. You may want to name the two teams as demonstrated in The Risk Takers activity.

Give children construction paper and ask them to cut out shapes of rocks. You may want to have the rocks pre-cut to save time. Place about 30 to 50 rocks randomly in the room so they resemble rocks in a river.

Invite children to use their imagination and pretend they are a super hero team and must cross this river to find success and happiness. Tell them that there are negative-thinking alligators in this river and their only hope to keep the alligators from eating their toes is to think positively.

Inviting one team member at a time, ask each child to attempt crossing Alligator River by saying one positive thought about themselves or others each time they step on a rock.

Turn the hour glass over and invite the children to challenge themselves to cross Alligator River before the sand runs out.

If a child cannot think of anything to say, invite group members to help think of ideas. As each super hero crosses Alligator River encourage the group to cheer and clap as loud as they can.

DISCUSSION

Children can learn at an early age about total behavior, that they have control over their thinking, and can choose to act on thoughts that are positive. Ask children to think of what they can do to help them stay away from negative thoughts. An example is to choose to play with children who are positive and do not choose negative actions or negative thinking.

CHOICES

Children can find other ways to cross Alligator River by presenting things they do well, people who love them, or effective choices they have made. This will help children learn more about themselves and their basic needs.

HAPPYWORK

Ask children to write one positive thing about themselves in their Happy Journal each day. Send home a Family Gram to help parents understand the significance of children learning how to substitute positive thoughts for negative thoughts. Encourage parents to remind children to write in their journal.

 Notes

I Was So Mad!

Purpose To learn to make effective choices when we are angry

Materials Two balloons per child, a pin, and "The Angry Story"

Time 45 minutes for activity

INSTRUCTIONS

Ask children to choose two balloons. Read the "The Angry Story" (see Resource Section) and ask them to participate.

Each time you read something in the story that would get the children angry (illustrated by a *), ask them to repeat in unison, "I WAS SO MAD!" At the same time, ask them to blow a small amount of air into their balloons.

Continue to read and follow the cues (*) until the balloons are ready to pop. When you give the final signal, tell the children to yell as loudly as they can "I Was So Mad That I Busted!" At this time, pop each child's balloon with a pin.

Take time to discuss anger and how we are similar to the balloon (see Discussion).

After the discussion, ask each child to blow air into their second balloon. Read the story again. This time, at the appropriate cues (*), encourage each child to take a turn saying "I was so mad, but I chose to _____."

Invite the child to select one of the effective choices for dealing with anger on the list (see Discussion). At the same time, ask all group members to release a little air out of their balloons. This time, at the finish of the story, there will be little air left in the balloons.

DISCUSSION

This is an effective activity to illustrate how we all get angry and what happens when we choose to let it build up inside. Make a list of all the people they know or know of (TV., cartoon and movie characters, etc.) who get angry. Explain to them that the only difference with all of us is how we choose to act out our anger. Ask the children to help you list all the ways they could choose to act out their anger, for example, hitting, cussing, sulking, calling names, etc. List these on a board or newsprint. Then ask children to help you think of effective ways to act out anger, for example, talk to someone, write down feelings, hit a pillow, etc. List these and display them for children to refer to during the second reading of the story.

CHOICES

Anger Role Play: Ask children to act out choices, both effective and ineffective, in a skit or a role play.

Ask children to use the Quality Interview activity to discover how others choose to act on their anger.

HAPPYWORK

Send home a Family Gram to tell parents the purpose of this activity. Encourage children to take the "The Angry Story" home and ask a parent to read the story to them. Ask children to practice what they learned in the group by stating "I WAS SO MAD, BUT I CHOSE TO _____" at the designated spot. Ask parents to applaud their child for their effective choices.

✎ **Notes**

Total Behavior Game

Purpose To explore total behavior and our thinking and doing choices

Materials Construction paper, markers, flip chart or blackboard

Time 45 minutes for activity and discussion

INSTRUCTIONS

Invite children to challenge themselves to think of as many feelings as they can, for example, sad, angry, happy, scared, etc. List them on a flip chart or blackboard.

Ask each child to choose one of the feelings listed and to draw picture on a sheet of construction paper of things that "make" them feel that way. Encourage children to write the name of that feeling on the paper and present it to the group.

After the discussion, asks group members to put their papers on the floor. Ask each child "How would you feel if _____? (i.e. someone stole your bike, someone teased you, someone gave you a present, you helped someone else) Encourage children to go stand on the paper that represents the feeling they chose.

Once the child is standing on their chosen square, ask these questions:

- What other feelings could you have chosen?
- When you have that feeling, what do you think? What do you do?
- When you have that feeling, what else could you think?
  What else could you do?

DISCUSSION

Children at an early age can learn about total behavior, that they have some control over their feelings, and can choose thoughts and actions that help them feel better. Ask children to think of other total behaviors they can choose to help them stay away from ineffective actions when they feel bad. Children also can begin to recognize positive and negative signals and they can choose how to act on those signals.

CHOICES

Share Your Feelings: Ask the children to make an envelope by folding one piece of construction paper in half and stapling it together. Ask the children to draw pictures of themselves on their envelopes. Encourage group members to write down on index cards all the feelings that they can remember experiencing in their lives and place the cards in their envelopes. Talk about what happens when too many feelings get into the envelope. Ask questions comparable to the questions used in the Total Behavior Game. (45 minutes for activity and discussion)

HAPPYWORK

Send home a Family Gram to tell parents the purpose of this exercise. Encourage children to write in their Happy Journals when they get a positive or negative feeling and what they chose to think or do that helped. Invite children to share what they have recorded in their Happy Journals with the group.

✎ **Notes**

Problem Solving

The Brain Game

Purpose   To understand that we always have choices when finding a solution to a problem

Materials   Flip chart or erasable board

Time   10 minutes per child

INSTRUCTIONS

Draw a big head or brain on a flip chart or erasable board. Write above the BRAIN, "A problem I have - These are some solutions." Section the head or BRAIN in half.

Ask one child to tell you a worry or concern that they may be choosing to think about. List this concern or worry in one half of the BRAIN.

Invite the group to challenge themselves to think of ways their group member can choose to take some effective control of this problem. Ask the child with the concern to join in the brainstorming session. List choices in the other half of the BRAIN.

After all the suggestions are offered, ask the child with the concern to choose a plan or develop their own.

Ask them to write their plan in their Happy Journal and to make a commitment to the group members to carry it out.

Allow each child to evaluate their plan with the group members at the next meeting, if they choose to do so.

DISCUSSION

This activity is an introduction to effective problem solving. The leader is actually modeling how to problem-solve by stating the problem, exploring options, evaluating options, and choosing a solution. Encourage children to offer options that are dependent on the doer, that encourage children to start doing something new, and that can be evaluated. More than one meeting may be necessary to explore problem solving.

CHOICES

Section the BRAIN into as many compartments as you have group members. Ask each child to share a worry or concern that they are experiencing. Fill up each compartment with one concern for each child. Ask group members to prioritize each concern and problem-solve one at a time. Draw additional BRAINS to list solutions for each child's problem.

Problem Box: Ask children to write problems on small slips of paper and place them in a shoe box. You may want to have these statements already prepared. Invite each child to choose a problem and ask group members to think of solutions.

Role Play: Encourage children to act out problems and find solutions.

HAPPYWORK

Ask each child to write their plan in their Happy Journal and act on it. If confidentiality is not an issue, it may be helpful to send home a Family Gram to help family members support the child's plan.

✎ <u>Notes</u>

Freedom Finder Planes

Purpose   To explore the need for freedom and how to meet this need

Materials   Notebook or typing paper, pencils, flip chart

Time   20 minutes to make and discuss planes

INSTRUCTIONS

Ask the children to help you make a list of all the places they would go if they had the choice. Make a list on a flip chart or blackboard for all to see.

Ask children to write down one of these places on a piece of paper, fold it into a Freedom Finder Plane, and fly their plane into the middle of the room.

Invite children to talk about what they wrote on their planes and proceed with the discussion.

DISCUSSION

This is an excellent activity to demonstrate that we all have unique pictures or wants in our quality worlds. To clarify how important pictures are ask:

"If you reached your destination, what would you have then that you don't have now (more Love - Power - Freedom - Fun)?"

Usually the destination is not obtainable at this time. We recommend that you ask:

"Are there any choices that you can make that will help you get some of what you really want today?"

Encouraging children to think about these needs can help them to begin planning to get some of their needs met today. This is also an opportunity to discuss the value of setting goals.

CHOICES

Instead of Freedom Finder Planes, substitute a Magic Wand, Aladdin's Lamp, Wishing Well, or any symbol that encourages children to think about their needs.

Dream Clouds: Ask children to create white clouds using white construction paper, markers, and scissors. Ask children to write or draw on the clouds dreams that they would like to see come true. Facilitate discussion with the group focusing on plans or goals to help their dreams come true. (Time: 30 minutes)

HAPPYWORK

Encourage children to ask a family member these two questions:

> Where would you choose to go if you had all the money in the world?
> As you don't have all that money, what do you choose to do instead?

Invite them to write in their Happy Journals. Send home a Family Gram to explain the objectives of this activity.

 Notes

Super Hero Cartoons

Purpose   To experience that helping someone is need-fulfilling

Materials   Construction paper, markers, cartoon frame

Time   45 minutes to draw and discuss cartoons

INSTRUCTIONS

Ask the children to think about someone they know who needs help with a particular problem or task. These problems could range from a friend who is being teased to a family member who need help around the house.

List all the ideas on the board and ask each child to pick one for their Super Hero cartoon character.

Ask children to draw the following using the four segment cartoon frame in the Resource section:

1. Super Hero looks for a person who needs help
2. Super Hero asks the person if they can help
3. Super Hero helps the other person
4. Super Hero walks away stating how they feel

Invite children to share their cartoons with the group members.

DISCUSSION

This exercise is an opportunity for you to discuss with children what is need-fulfilling about helping others. Ask questions such as:

- How is it need-fulfilling for a person that is helped?
- How is it need-fulfilling for you to help someone else?

Introduce the concept of *pictures* by asking the children if they can picture themselves doing the same things as their Super Heroes In this activity concentrate on total behavior. Children are thinking about a problem, making a choice to do something about it, and feeling differently after they have followed through with their plan. Discuss with children how they feel after they have made an effective choice and follow it through.

CHOICES

Use this activity with The Risk Takers activity. Super Hero cartoons can depict children acting on the world in a number of effective ways such as working out their own problems, taking a risk, or learning a new skill.

HAPPYWORK

Encourage children to go out into the world and be a Super Hero and help someone. Be sure to remember to send a Family Gram to help parents understand the purpose of this activity. Invite them to share any positive experiences with the group.

✎ **Notes**

The Risk Takers

Purpose To introduce taking risks to solve problems

Materials Paper and pens

Time 30 minutes to draw, present, and discuss

INSTRUCTIONS

Tell the children that you are starting a new super heroes TV show called "The Risk Takers." The heroes have worries and concerns, but always take risks and figure out solutions to their problems. Ask them to help you develop plots for each show by sharing a problem they are having.

Ask the children to imagine themselves as one of the Risk Takers and encourage them to draw a picture of themselves working out the problem. Drawings might illustrate them talking to someone with whom they are having a conflict, working hard to get a better grade on a test, trying out for a sports team, etc.

After each child has completed a picture, ask them to help their new heroes by listing the steps a Risk Taker character would have to do and think to solve their problem.

DISCUSSION

Risk taking is a skill that successful and happy people have learned to add to their lives. This activity introduces risk taking in a fun and non-threatening way. Encourage children to think of a name for their group and a theme or goal to go with the name.

CHOICES

Super Hero Spectacular: Other hero shows can be developed with the help of group members. The Problem Solvers, The Helpers, and The Happy Group are examples. Integrate this activity with the Super Hero Cartoon activity to help build a group theme.

Super Hero Teams: Invite children to name their team, but this time ask them to think of different ways to solve a problem as a group.

HAPPYWORK

Ask the children to practice some of their suggestions and ideas for their fictional super hero characters in situations they are experiencing in their lives. Encourage children to share what they learned from this activity with their families and with the group. Remember to send home a Family Gram.

Attack

Purpose To learn effective behavioral skills and self-control when others use negative behavior

Materials Flip chart or blackboard, video camera or tape player (optional)

Time 45 minutes for role play and discussion

INSTRUCTIONS

Invite the children to help you make a list of all the behaviors that they do not like other children to use, for example, teasing, yelling, cursing, ignoring, etc.

Ask children to choose one of the behaviors in the list. Tell them that you are going to demonstrate a skill that will help them know what to do when someone Attacks them using one of these behaviors. Tell them when they learn this skill, they truly will be a Super Hero.

Ask for a volunteer to role play the behavior. (Our behavior for this example will be "teasing.") Encourage your volunteer to tease you in the same way that they do not like to be teased.

Present and role model the strategy below for teasing:

Attacker	teases Super Hero.
Super Hero	says, "What are you doing?"
Attacker	will naturally pause or say what they are doing.
Super Hero	says, "What you are doing is teasing me and I don't like it. If you want to stop, I will stay. If you continue to tease, I will leave."

Ask them to practice over and over, substituting different behaviors.

DISCUSSION

This is a profound approach to helping children learn how to assert themselves in a way that they do not lose power or get into trouble. Let them know that this skill will take a little work and a lot of self-control. Demonstrate that when asking the question, "What are you doing?", the focus switches from them to the attacker. Further, by stating the behavior, ("What you are doing is teasing me and I don't like it.") the Super Hero has now defined the standards. Finally, when asserting ("If you want to stop, I will stay. If you continue to tease me, I will leave."), the Super Hero has given the attacker choices and has achieved equal status.

CHOICES

Use the buddy system and ask partners to practice this skill. Choose several behaviors and invite children to watch themselves manage all types of attacks.

HAPPYWORK

Send home a Family Gram to help parents understand the purpose of this activity. Be sure to outline the steps of Attack and encourage children to practice with their parents. It may help to send home an entire script for children and parents to read. Invite children to share their experiences with the group.

Notes

The Resources

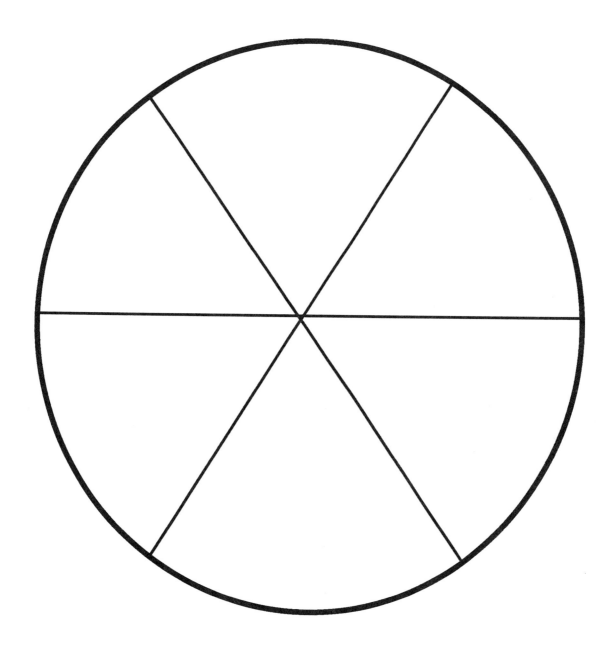

Buddy Mobile

Cheers and Raps

I am as nice as I can be. If you look at me someone happy you will see.

I like me. I am pretty cool. As a matter of fact, being cool is my rule.

I like me. I am very nice. I am as sweet as sugar and spice.

I like me. I like me. I am O.K. I hope you will see that's my way.

I like today. Hip hip hooray. If I may say, thinking happy is the way.

We are special, yes we are. We are super and a star.
We feel good about ourselves. We are proud and will go far.
We've the only one like us. Thinking happy is a must.

G-r-e-a-t. That means we are great, we are great in every way.

I once knew a girl who was very sad.
She was feeling blue and oh so bad.
So she asked her friend just what to do
Since she was feeling sad and blue.

Her friend said, "Hey, let's have some fun"
And jump and run and play today.
You see you're O.K. and you gotta say
I am great in every way.

And so this girl she started thinking
Every time she started sinking,
I'm O.K. and I'm gonna say
I am great in every way.

She felt much better
And the day I met her
She felt O.K. and had to say
Thinking happy is now my way.

Cheers

Guess Who?

1. What is your favorite ice cream?
2. What is one thing you do for fun?
3. What is your favorite food?
4. What is your favorite sport?
5. What is your favorite toy?
6. Name one thing you do well.
7. Name one person who loves you.
8. Name one person you care about.
9. What is one thing you do that makes you feel important?
10. What is your favorite candy bar?
11. What is your favorite subject in school?
12. What is your favorite restaurant to go to?
13. What is your favorite cartoon?
14. What is your favorite TV show?
15. Who is your favorite superhero?
16. What is your favorite color?
17. What is your favorite animal?
18. What is your favorite game to play?
19. If you could go anywhere in the world, where would you go?
20. What is your favorite fruit?
21. If you could give your mom anything in the world, what would it be?
22. What is your favorite holiday?
23. What is your least favorite holiday?
24. What is your favorite story?
25. What is one thing you like about yourself?
26. What is your least favorite thing about school?
27. What is your favorite thing to do outside?
28. What is your favorite day of the week?
29. What kind of pizza do you like best?
30. What kind of cookies do you like best?
31. Who is your favorite singer?
32. What is your favorite kind of dance?
33. What is your favorite thing to do with your family?
34. What is your favorite chore to do at home?
35. What is your least favorite chore to do at home?
36. What is your favorite …?
37. What is your favorite number?
38. What is your favorite car?
39. What is something you do well?
40. What is your least favorite color?
41. What is one food you do not like to eat?
42. What is your favorite song?
43. What is your favorite vegetable?
44. What is your favorite season?
45. What is your favorite time of the school day?
46. What is your favorite kind of bubble gum?
47. What is your favorite time of the day?
48. What is your best sport?
49. Who is someone that makes you feel special?
50. What is your favorite pet ?

Guess Who?

The Angry Story

Once upon a time there was a little girl named _____(you may use the name of a child in the group to personalize the story). _____was in the _____ grade (insert average grade of children in the group). One morning, as _____ was sleeping , her mother rushed into_____ 's room to wake her up. "Get up, _____!" said her mother in a very loud voice. Although _____ heard her mother talking, she kept laying in the bed. It was usually very hard for _____ to get up, especially when she had stayed up late the night before watching a movie. It wasn't long before _____ 's mom realized that _____ wasn't up and she started screaming very loudly, "Get up out of that bed and I mean now!" _____ knew when her mom meant business and she jumped out of bed so fast that she stumped her toe and hit her knee on the bedside table. *(Group repeats: "I was so mad!")

_____ hurried to get dressed and ran to the kitchen to eat breakfast. As she picked up the glass of orange juice,_____ accidentally spilled the whole glass on the floor. Her mom was in a really bad mood by now and yelled to _____, "No TV. this afternoon young lady. I've told you to be more careful. You are so clumsy. You can't do anything right!" *(Group repeats: "I was so mad!") This day was not going well so far.

Then it was time to catch the bus. _____ hoped the rest of the day would be better, but still felt a little angry inside because of the rough morning. _____ was one of the last kids to get on the bus and this day she had to take the worst seat of all. It was the one right beside Sam, the biggest bully on the bus. As_____ 's luck would have it, Sam started picking on her right away. Finally, she was feeling so mad, she just hauled off and hit him so hard he almost fell off the seat. Of course _____hit him just as the bus driver turned around to look at her. Guess who the bus driver saw hitting — _____ , of course. Guess who got a conduct slip, _____ of course! Guess who had to see the principal — _____ , of course. *(Group repeats: "I was so mad!")

I was so Mad!

Then she finally got to her class and put all her things in her desk. _____ was still feeling really mad inside. Then Leon, another student in the class came right over to her and snatched her pencil right out of her hand. Of course, _____ grabbed it back and said, "Give me back my pencil or I'll tell the teacher on you!" Unfortunately, the teacher heard her and put her name on the board. The teacher said she was disrupting the class and that she had a "bad attitude." *(Group repeats: "I was so mad!")

Then at snack time, _____ realized that she had forgotten her snack. *(Group repeats: "I was so mad!") By now, _____ was so mad that she just didn't know what to do with all of the mad feelings inside.

So, _____ decided to go play in the computer center. Along came Emily and asked _____ to play but _____ was in such a bad mood that she did not want to talk or play with anyone. But Emily kept insisting and talking in that silly voice that she talks in sometimes. Then when _____ got up to ask the teacher a question, Emily sat right down in "her" spot. When she got back, she was so mad at her for taking "her" spot that she reached over and pushed her right on the floor. *(Group repeats: "I was so mad I busted!" Pop balloon.) Then Emily was crying, the teacher was yelling, and _____ was going to the principal's office. Boy, what a bad day _____ had and all because of those mad feelings.

I was so Mad!

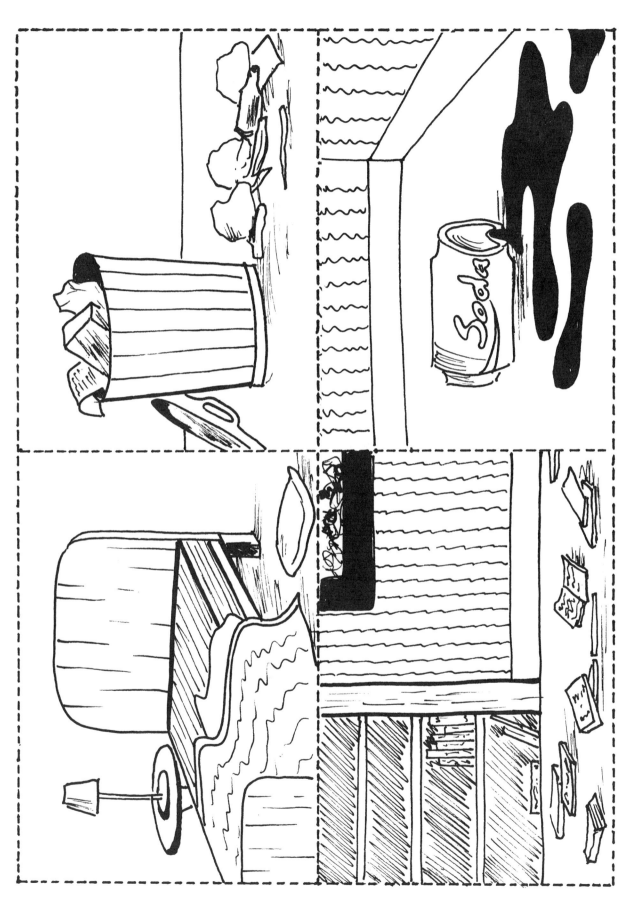

Helping Game

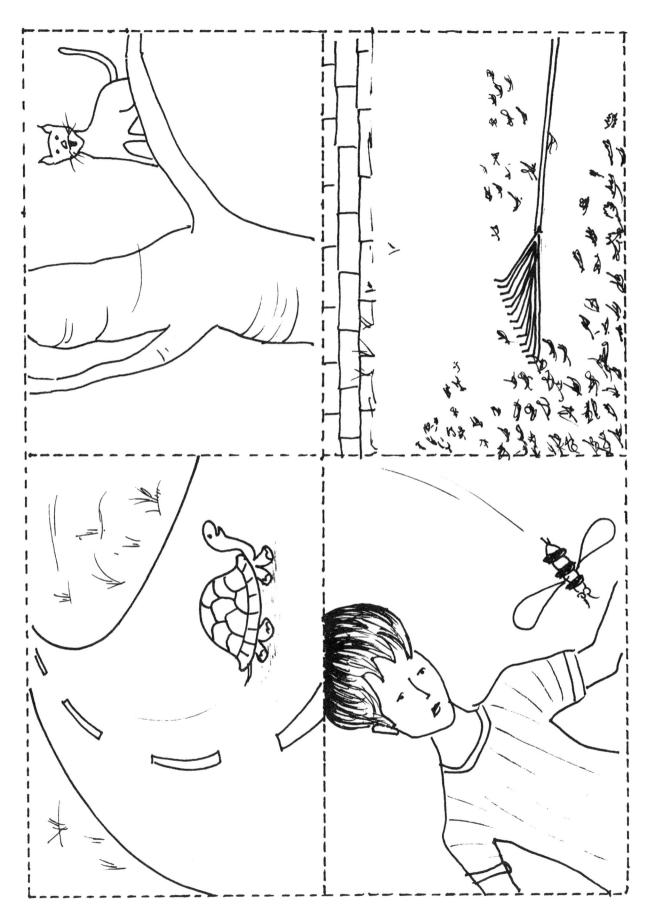

Helping Game

Happy Mobiles

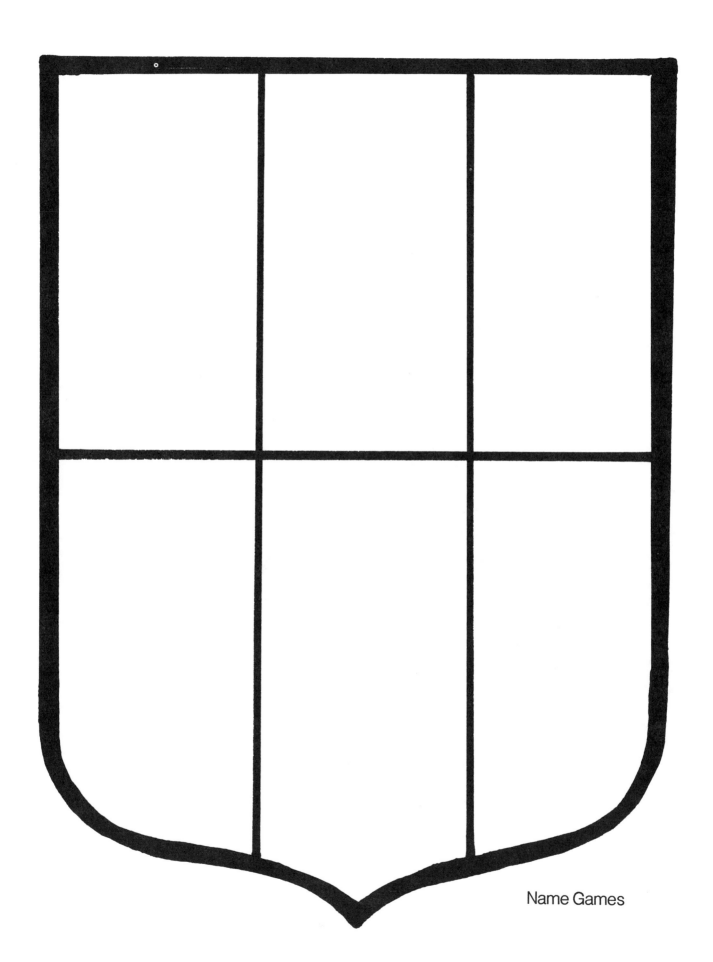

Name Games

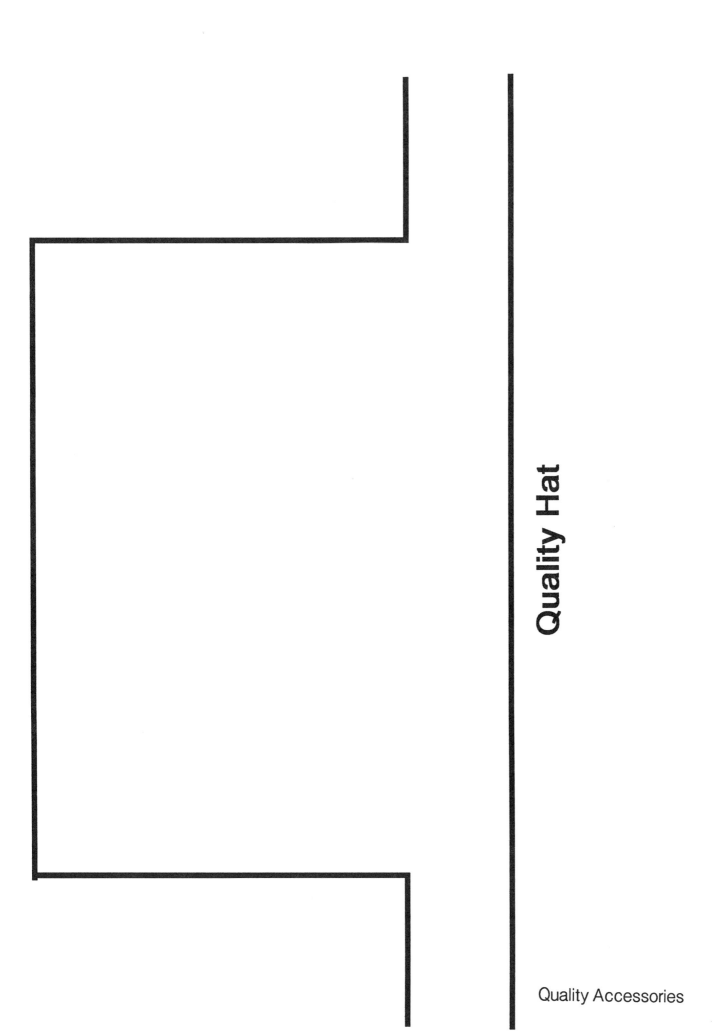

Quality Clothespins

Quality Clothespins

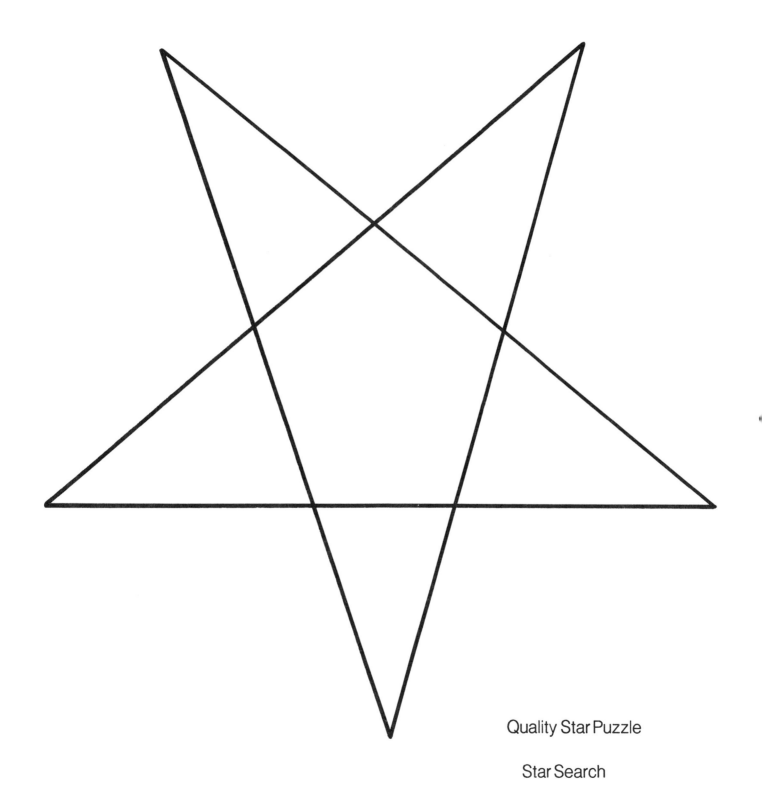

Quality Star Puzzle

Star Search

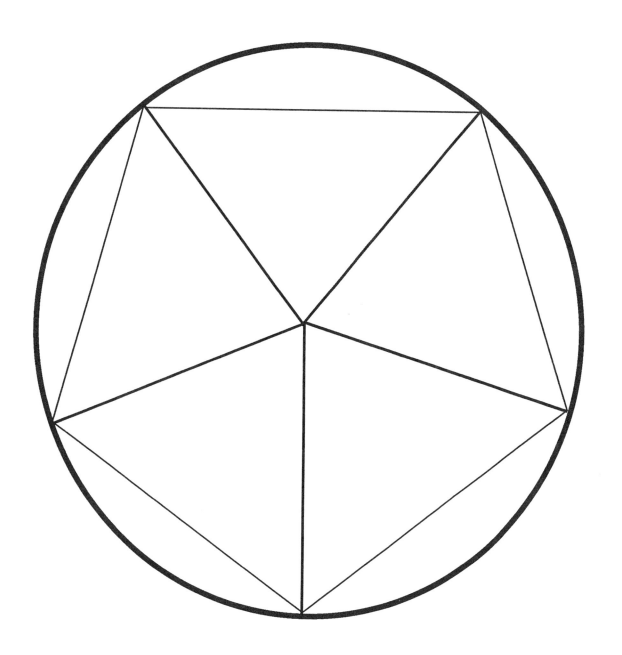

Quality Star Puzzle: Quality Circle

S	M	I	L	E
1 WONDERFUL	11 GOOD	21 COOL	31 FRIENDLY	41 CREATIVE
2 HAPPY	12 JOYFUL	22 CARING	32 SPECIAL	42 COURAGE
3 IMPORTANT	13 FAIR	23 SHARING	33 GIVE	43 GRATEFUL
4 BRAVE	14 EXCELLENT	24 BEAUTIFUL	34 DEPENDABLE	44 MOTIVATED
5 NICE	15 SHARE	25 LIKE	35 GLAD	45 DETERMINED

Smile Bingo

S M I L E

S	M	I	L	E
6 GREAT	**16** PLEASANT	**26** KIND	**36** TRUSTWORTHY	**46** FABULOUS
7 COOPERATIVE	**17** STRONG	**27** FORGIVING	**37** RESPONSIBLE	**47** GIVING
8 LOVE	**18** WELL-MANNERED	**28** GREAT	**38** HELPER	**48** SENSITIVE
9 BOLD	**19** HELPFUL	**29** HONEST	**39** LEADER	**49** TOLERANT
10 TERRIFIC	**20** PRECIOUS	**30** WORKER	**40** EXCITED	**50** PATIENT

Smile Bingo

Smile Bingo

Card 1

S	M	I	L	E
1 WONDERFUL	12 JOYFUL	26 KIND	40 EXCITED	49 TOLERANT
4 BRAVE	13 FAIR	30 WORKER	39 LEADER	50 PATIENT
7 COOPERATIVE	11 GOOD	27 FORGIVING	36 TRUST-WORTHY	47 GIVING
5 NICE	19 HELPFUL	21 COOL	35 GLAD	48 SENSITIVE
9 BOLD	18 WELL-MANNERED	29 HONEST	31 FRIENDLY	44 MOTIVATED

Card 2

S	M	I	L	E
2 HAPPY	13 FAIR	30 WORKER	31 FRIENDLY	43 GRATEFUL
4 BRAVE	16 PLEASANT	26 KIND	40 EXCITED	42 COURAGE
10 TERRIFIC	14 EXCELLENT	23 SHARING	37 RESPONSIBLE	48 SENSITIVE
9 BOLD	17 STRONG	29 HONEST	36 TRUST-WORTHY	45 DETERMINED
3 IMPORTANT	11 GOOD	22 CARING	39 LEADER	47 GIVING

S	M	I	L	E	S	M	I	L	E
5 NICE	20 PRECIOUS	26 KIND	38 HELPER	50 PATIENT	6 GREAT	14 EXCELLENT	24 BEAUTIFUL	32 SPECIAL	41 CREATIVE
7 COOPERATIVE	19 HELPFUL	25 LIKE	33 GIVE	49 TOLERANT	3 IMPORTANT	19 HELPFUL	26 KIND	37 RESPONSIBLE	46 FABULOUS
8 LOVE	12 JOYFUL	30 WORKER	32 SPECIAL	46 FABULOUS	8 LOVE	16 PLEASANT	23 SHARING	38 HELPER	42 COURAGE
6 GREAT	18 WELL-MANNERED	27 FORGIVING	35 GLAD	41 CREATIVE	2 HAPPY	17 STRONG	25 LIKE	34 DEPENDABLE	43 GRATEFUL
1 WONDERFUL	15 SHARE	24 BEAUTIFUL	34 DEPENDABLE	44 MOTIVATED	10 TERRIFIC	15 SHARE	22 CARING	33 GIVE	45 DETERMINED

Smile Bingo

Smile Bingo

S	M	I	L	E	S	M	I	L	E
1 WONDERFUL	17 STRONG	26 KIND	34 DEPENDABLE	47 GIVING	6 GREAT	13 FAIR	29 HONEST	35 GLAD	46 FABULOUS
6 GREAT	12 JOYFUL	29 HONEST	32 SPECIAL	45 DETERMINED	9 BOLD	15 SHARE	22 CARING	33 GIVE	43 GRATEFUL
4 BRAVE	20 PRECIOUS	30 WORKER	35 GLAD	46 FABULOUS	5 NICE	14 EXCELLENT	21 COOL	34 DEPENDABLE	45 DETERMINED
5 NICE	16 PLEASANT	27 FORGIVING	36 TRUST-WORTHY	43 GRATEFUL	7 COOPERATIVE	16 PLEASANT	27 FORGIVING	36 TRUST-WORTHY	48 SENSITIVE
3 IMPORTANT	13 FAIR	24 BEAUTIFUL	33 GIVE	44 MOTIVATED	10 TERRIFIC	17 STRONG	26 KIND	32 SPECIAL	44 MOTIVATED

Smile Bingo

S	M	I	L	E
9 BOLD	17 STRONG	21 COOL	32 SPECIAL	48 SENSITIVE
8 LOVE	13 FAIR	26 KIND	31 FRIENDLY	49 TOLERANT
5 NICE	19 HELPFUL	29 HONEST	33 GIVE	41 CREATIVE
4 BRAVE	15 SHARE	27 FORGIVING	38 HELPER	43 GREATEFUL
2 HAPPY	14 EXCELLENT	30 WORKER	39 LEADER	42 COURAGE

S	M	I	L	E
9 BOLD	16 PLEASANT	27 FORGIVING	39 LEADER	48 SENSITIVE
2 HAPPY	14 EXCELLENT	22 CARING	34 DEPENDABLE	43 GRATEFUL
1 WONDERFUL	17 STRONG	23 SHARING	32 SPECIAL	50 PATIENT
3 IMPORTANT	15 SHARE	29 HONEST	26 KIND	49 TOLERANT
10 TERRIFIC	18 WELL-MANNERED	30 WORKER	31 FRIENDLY	45 DETERMINED

Smile Bingo Card 1

S	M	I	L	E
8 LOVE	19 HELPFUL	21 COOL	37 RESPONSIBLE	42 COURAGE
7 COOPERATIVE	13 FAIR	25 LIKE	36 TRUST-WORTHY	47 GIVING
5 NICE	11 GOOD	24 BEAUTIFUL	35 GLAD	44 MOTIVATED
4 BRAVE	20 PRECIOUS	26 KIND	33 GIVE	41 CREATIVE
6 GREAT	12 JOYFUL	20 PRECIOUS	38 HELPER	46 FABULOUS

Smile Bingo Card 2

S	M	I	L	E
7 COOPERATIVE	12 JOYFUL	23 SHARING	34 DEPENDABLE	45 DETERMINED
1 WONDERFUL	11 GOOD	22 CARING	35 GLAD	44 MOTIVATED
6 GREAT	16 PLEASANT	25 LIKE	40 EXCITED	46 FABULOUS
3 IMPORTANT	20 PRECIOUS	24 BEAUTIFUL	36 TRUST-WORTHY	50 PATIENT
10 TERRIFIC	18 WELL-MANNERED	26 KIND	37 RESPONSIBLE	47 GIVING

Smile Bingo

SMILE Bingo Card 1

S	M	I	L	E
3 IMPORTANT	19 HELPFUL	30 WORKER	37 RESPONSIBLE	47 GIVING
4 BRAVE	20 PRECIOUS	25 LIKE	38 HELPER	50 PATIENT
2 HAPPY	18 WELL-MANNERED	23 SHARING	39 LEADER	42 COURAGE
8 LOVE	12 JOYFUL	24 BEAUTIFUL	31 FRIENDLY	49 TOLERANT
1 WONDERFUL	11 GOOD	26 KIND	40 EXCITED	41 CREATIVE

SMILE Bingo Card 2

S	M	I	L	E
1 WONDERFUL	11 GOOD	25 LIKE	38 HELPER	49 TOLERANT
10 TERRIFIC	18 WELL-MANNERED	26 KIND	37 RESPONSIBLE	48 SENSITIVE
8 LOVE	15 SHARE	23 SHARING	39 LEADER	42 COURAGE
6 GREAT	19 HELPFUL	22 CARING	31 FRIENDLY	41 CREATIVE
2 HAPPY	14 EXCELLENT	21 COOL	40 EXCITED	50 PATIENT

Smile Bingo

Super Hero sees someone
who needs help.

Super Hero asks the person,
"May I help?"

Super Hero walks away and says, "I feel ___."

Super Hero helps the other person.

Bibliography

The following references are materials we have consulted in compiling some of these ideas. To be certain, this list is not complete. We have picked up some of the ideas throughout the years through various workshops, teachers, counselors, and colleagues.

Frey, Diane and C. Jesse Carlock, *Enhancing Self-Esteem,*
      Accelerated Development, Inc., 1989.
Good, E. Perry, *Happy Hour Guide,*
      New View Publications, 1989.
Good, E. Perry, *In Pursuit of Happiness,*
      New View Publications, 1989.
Phillips, Deborah, *How to give your Child A Great Self-Esteem,*
      Random House, 1989.
From the editors of Group Publishing, Group Growers,
      Thom Schultz Publications, Inc., 1988.
Borva, Michele and Craig, *Self-Esteem: A Classroom Affair,*
      Harper and Row Publishers, 1988.
Hallinan, P.K, *I'm Glad To Be Me,*
      Children's Press, Chicago, 1977.
Muntean, Michaela, *The Little Engine That Could,*
      Platt and Munk Publishers, 1988.
Pumsey, *In Pursuit of Excellence and Bright Beginnings,*
      Timberline Press.
Sullo, Robert A., *Teach Them To Be Happy,*
      New View Publications, 1989.
Borba, Dr. Michele, *Esteem Builders,*
      Jalmar Press, California, 1989.
Kirchner, Glenn, *Physical Education for Elementary School Children,*
      William C. Brown Publishers, 1985.

Additional Resources:

Bowman, Dr. Bob, *Workshop on Motivation Students at Risk,*
      Professor, University of South Carolina.
1991-92 *Elementary Drug Curriculum Guide*
Carr, Tom, Ideas from Student Services Workshop, 1991.